DATE DUE

MAY 6 1988			
MAY 1 6 1989			
MAR 2 0 1990			
SEP 1 8 1991			
APR 5 - 1996			
JUN 1 1 2002			
APR 2 5 2004			

AT THE SIGN
OF THE BARBER'S POLE

REVIEWS OF PREVIOUS BOOKS

"Valuable and interesting."—*The Times.*

"A fascinating work."—*Whitehall Review.*

"Mr Andrews' book does not contain a dull page. . . . Deserves to meet with a warm welcome."—*Yorkshire Post.*

"This is an entertaining book."—*The Athenæum.*

"Mr Andrews' books are always interesting."—*Church Bells.*

"A most delightful work."—*Leeds Mercury.*

"Mr Andrews has the true art of narration, and contrives to give us the results of his learning wich considerable freshness of style, while his subjects are always interesting and picturesque."—*Manchester Courier.*

"No student of Mr Andrews' books can be a dull after-dinner speaker, for his writings are full of curious out-of-the-way information and good stories."—*Birmingham Daily Gazette.*

"It is chatty and instructive from cover to cover."—*The Antiquary.*

"Most pleasantly readable."—*Yorkshire Herald.*

"Mr Andrews not only writes with enthusiasm for his subject, but has arranged and marshalled his facts and figures with great skill, and produced a thoroughly popular work, that will be eagerly read and with advantage."—*Society.*

"A volume full of valuable information well and pleasantly put."—*London Quarterly Review.*

The House of Commons in the time of Sir Robert Walpole.
Wigs in Parliament.

AT THE SIGN
OF THE BARBER'S POLE

STUDIES IN HIRSUTE HISTORY

BY

WILLIAM ANDREWS

AUTHOR OF "BYGONE ENGLAND"
ETC.

COTTINGHAM, YORKSHIRE
J. R. TUTIN
1904

Detroit: Reissued by Singing Tree Press, Book Tower, 1969

Library of Congress Catalog Card Number 74-77164

PREFACE

ONNECTED with the barber and his calling are many curiosities of history. In the following pages, an attempt has been made, and I trust not without success, to bring together notices of the more interesting matters that gather round the man and his trade.

In the compilation of this little book many works have been consulted, and among those which have yielded me the most information must be mentioned the following :—

"Annals of the Barber-Surgeons of London," by Sidney Young, London, 1890.

"An Apology for the Beard," by Artium Magister, London, 1862.

"Barbers' Company," by G. Lambert, F.S.A., London, 1881.

"Barber-Surgeons and Chandlers," by D. Embleton, M.D., Newcastle-on-Tyne, 1891.

"Barber's Shop," by R. W. Proctor, edited by W. E. A. Axon, Manchester, 1883.

"Philosophy of Beards," by T. S. Cowing, Ipswich.

"Some Account of the Beard and the

Moustachio," by John Adey Repton,
F.S.A., London, 1839.

"Why Shave?" by H. M., London.

Notes and Queries, and other periodicals, as
well as encyclopædias, books on costume, and
old plays, have been drawn upon, and numerous
friends have supplied me with information. I
must specially mention with gratitude Mr Everard
Home Coleman, the well-known contributor to
Notes and Queries.

Some of my chapters have been previously
published in the magazines, but all have been
carefully revised and additions have been made
to them.

In conclusion, I hope this work will prove a
welcome contribution to the byways of history.

WILLIAM ANDREWS.

Royal Institution, Hull,
August 11th, 1904.

CONTENTS

LIST OF ILLUSTRATIONS

THE BARBER'S POLE

IN most instances the old signs which indicated the callings of shopkeepers have been swept away. Indeed, the three brass balls of the pawn-broker and the pole of the barber are all that are left of signs of the olden time. Round the barber's pole gather much curious fact and fiction. So many suggestions have been put forth as to its origin and meaning that the student of history is puzzled to give a correct solution. One circumstance is clear : its origin goes back to far distant times. An attempt is made in " The Athenian Oracle " (i. 334), to trace the remote origin of the pole. " The barber's art," says the book, " was so beneficial to the publick, that he who first brought it up in Rome had, as authors relate, a statue erected to his memory. In England they were in some sort the surgeons of old times, into whose art those beautiful leeches,[1] our fair virgins, were also ac-customed to be initiated. In cities and corporate towns they still retain their name Barber-Chirurgions. They therefore used to hang their

[1] This is the old word for doctors or surgeons.

basons out upon poles to make known at a distance to the weary and wounded traveller where all might have recourse. They used poles, as some inns still gibbet their signs, across a town." It is a doubtful solution of the origin of the barber's sign.

A more satisfactory explanation is given in the "Antiquarian Repertory." "The barber's pole," it is there stated, "has been the subject of many conjectures, some conceiving it to have originated from the word poll or head, with several other conceits far-fetched and as unmeaning; but the true intention of the party coloured staff was to show that the master of the shop practised surgery and could breathe a vein as well as mow a beard: such a staff being to this day by every village practitioner put in the hand of the patient undergoing the operation of phlebotomy. The white band, which encompasses the staff, was meant to represent the fillet thus elegantly twined about it." We reproduce a page from "Comenii Orbis Pictus," perhaps better known under its English title of the "Visible World." It is said to have been the first illustrated school-book printed, and was published in 1658. Comenius was born in 1592, was a Moravian bishop, a famous educational reformer, and the writer of many works, including the "Visible World: or a Nomenclature, and Pictures of all the chief things that are in the World, and of Men's Employments therein; in above an 150 Copper

The Barber, 1.
in the Barbers-shop, 2.
cutteth off the Hair
and the Beard
with a pair of Sizzars, 3.
or shaveth with a Razor,
which he taketh out of his
Case, 4.
And he washeth one
over a Bason, 5.
with Suds running
out of a Laver, 6.
and also with Sope, 7.
and wipeth him
with a Towel, 8.
combeth him with a Comb, 9.
and curleth him
with a Crisping Iron, 10.
Sometimes he cutteth a Vein
with a Pen-knife, 11.
where the Blood spirteth out, 12.

Tonsor, 1.
in *Tonstrina,* 2.
tondet *Crines*
& *Barbam*
Forcipe, 3.
vel radit *Novacula,*
quam è *Theca,* 4. depromit.

Et lavat
super *Pelvim,* 5.
Lixivio defluente
è *Gutturnio,* 6.
ut & *Sapone,* 7.
& tergit
Linteo, 8.
pectit *Pectine,* 9.
crispat
Calamistro, 10.
Interdum Venam secat
Scalpello, 11.
ubi Sanguis propullulat, 12.
The

The Barber's Shop, from "Orbis Pictus."

Cuts." Under each picture are explanatory sentences in two columns, one in Latin, and the other in English, and by this means the pupil in addition to learning Latin, was able to gain much useful knowledge respecting industries and other " chief things that are in the World." For a century this was the most popular text-book in Europe, and was translated into not fewer than fourteen languages. It has been described as a crude effort to interest the young, and it was more like an illustrated dictionary than a child's reading-book. In the picture of the interior of a barber's shop, a patient is undergoing the operation of phlebotomy (figure 11). He holds in his hand a pole or staff having a bandage twisted round it. It is stated in Brand's " Popular Antiquities " that an illustration in a missal of the time of Edward the First represents this ancient practice.

In a speech made in the House of Peers by Lord Thurlow, in support of postponing the further reading of the Surgeons' Incorporation Bill, from July 17th, 1797, to that day three months, the noble lord said that by a statute still in force, the barbers and surgeons were each to use a pole. The barbers were to have theirs blue and white, striped, with no other appendage ; but the surgeon's pole, which was the same in other respects, was likewise to have a galley-pot and a red rag, to denote the particular nature of their vocation.

A question is put in the *British Apollo* (London, 1708) :—

> ". . . Why a barber at port-hole
> Puts forth a party-coloured pole ? "

This is the answer given :—

> " In ancient Rome, when men lov'd fighting,
> And wounds and scars took much delight in,
> Man-menders then had noble pay,
> Which we call surgeons to this day.
> 'Twas order'd that a hughe long pole,
> With bason deck'd should grace the hole,
> To guide the wounded, who unlopt
> Could walk, on stumps the others hopt ;
> But, when they ended all their wars,
> And men grew out of love with scars,
> Their trade decaying ; to keep swimming
> They joyn'd the other trade of trimming,
> And on their poles to publish either,
> Thus twisted both their trades together."

During his residence at his living in the county of Meath, before he was advanced to the deanery of St Patrick's, Dean Swift was daily shaved by the village barber, who gained his esteem. The barber one morning, when busy lathering Swift, said he had a great favour to ask his reverence, adding that at the suggestion of his neighbours he had taken a small public-house at the corner of the churchyard. He hoped that with the two businesses he might make a better living for his family.

" Indeed," said the future Dean, " and what can I do to promote the happy union ? "

"And please you," said the barber, "some of our customers have heard much about your reverence's poetry ; so that, if you would but condescend to give me a smart little touch in that way to clap under my sign, it might be the making of me and mine for ever."

"But what do you intend for your sign ? " inquired the cleric.

"The ' Jolly Barber,' if it please your reverence, with a razor in one hand and a full pot in the other."

"Well," rejoined Swift, "in that case there can be no great difficulty in supplying you with a suitable inscription." Taking up a pen he instantly wrote the following couplet, which was duly painted on the sign and remained there for many years :—

"Rove not from pole to pole, but step in here,
    Where nought excels the shaving but—the beer."

Another barber headed his advertisement with a parody on a couplet from Goldsmith as follows :—

"Man wants but little beard below,
    Nor wants that little long."

A witty Parisian hairdresser on one of the Boulevards put up a sign having on it a portrait of Absalom dangling by his hair from a tree, and Joab piercing his body with a spear. Under the painting was the following terse epigram :—

> " Passans, contemplez le malheur
>   D'Absalom pendu par la nuque ;
>   Il aurait evité ce malheur,
>   S'il eut porté une perruque."

The lines lose some of their piquancy when rendered into English as follows :—

> " The wretched Absalom behold,
>   Suspended by his flowing hair :
>   He might have 'scaped this hapless fate
>   Had he chosen a wig to wear."

THE BARBER'S SHOP

HE old-fashioned barber has passed away. In years agone he was a notable tradesman, and was a many-sided man of business, for he shaved, cut hair, made wigs, bled, dressed wounds, and performed other offices. When the daily papers were not in the hands of the people he retailed the current news, and usually managed to scent the latest scandal, which he was not slow to make known—in confidence, and in an under-tone, of course. He was an intelligent fellow, with wit as keen as his razor ; urbane, and having the best of tempers. It has been truth-fully said of this old-time tradesman that one might travel from pole to pole and never en-counter an ill-natured or stupid barber.

Long days are usually worked in the barber's shop, and many attempts have been made to reduce the hours of labour. We must not forget that compulsory early closing is by no means a new cry, as witness the following edict, issued in the reign of Henry VI., by the Reading Corporation : " Ordered that no barber open his shop to shave any man after 10 o'clock at night from Easter to Michaelmas, or 9 o'clock from Michaelmas to Easter, except it be any stranger or any worthy man of the town that hath need; whoever doeth to the contrary to pay one thousand tiles to the Guildhall."

In the reign of Queen Elizabeth the rich families from the country thought it no disgrace in that simple age to lodge in Fleet Street, or take rooms above some barber's shop. At this period, indeed, the barber-surgeon was a man of considerable importance. His shop was the gathering-place of idle gallants, who came to have their sword-wounds dressed after street frays. The gittern, or guitar, lay on the counter, and this was played by a customer to pass away the time until his turn came to have his hair trimmed, his beard starched, his mustachios curled, and his love-locks tied up. We give a picture of a barber's shop at this period ; the place appears more like a museum than an establishment for conducting business. We get a word picture of a barber's shop in Greene's " Quip for an Upstart Courtier," pub-

lished in 1592. It is related that the courtier
sat down in the throne of a chair, and the barber,
after saluting him with a low bow, would thus
address him : " Sir, will you have your worship's

A Barber's Shop in the Time of Queen Elizabeth.

hair cut after the Italian manner, short and
round, and then frounst with the curling irons
to make it look like a half-moon in a mist ; or
like a Spaniard, long at the ears and curled like
to the two ends of an old cast periwig ; or will

you be Frenchified with a love-lock down to
your shoulders, whereon you may wear your
mistress's favour? The English cut is base,
and gentlemen scorn it; novelty is dainty.
Speak the word, sir, my scissors are ready to
execute your worship's will." A couple of
hours were spent in combing and dressing the
ambrosial locks of the young Apollo; then the
barber's basin was washed with camphor soap.
At last the beard is reached, and with another
congee the barber asks if his worship would wish
it to be shaven; "whether he would have his
peak cut short and sharp, and amiable like an
inamorato, or broad pendent like a spade, to be
amorous as a lover or terrible as a warrior and
soldado; whether he will have his crates cut
low like a juniper bush, or his subercles taken
away with a razor; if it be his pleasure to have
his appendices primed, or his moustachios
fostered to turn about his ears like vine tendrils,
fierce and curling, or cut down to the lip with
the Italian lash?—and with every question a
snip of the scissors and a bow." If a poor man
entered the shop he was polled for twopence,
and was soon trimmed around like a cheese,
and dismissed with scarce a "God speed you."

The Puritans looked askance at the fashions
introduced by the barbers. No wonder when
the talk in the shop was about the French cut,
the Spanish cut, the Dutch and the Italian
mode; the bravado fashion, and the mean

style. In addition to these were the gentleman's cut, the common cut, the Court cut, and
county cut. " And," wrote Stubbes with indignation, " they have other kinds of cuts innumer-
able, and, therefore, when you come to be
trimmed they will ask you whether you will
be cut to look terrible to your enemy, or amiable to your friend ; grim and stern in countenance, or pleasant and demure ; for they have
diverse kinds of cuts for all these purposes, or
else they lie ! Then when they have done all
their feats, it is a world to consider how their
mowchatows must be preserved and laid out
from one cheek to another ; yea, almost from
one ear to another, and turned up like two
horns towards the forehead. Besides that,
when they come to the cutting of the hair,
what tricking and trimming, what rubbing,
what scratching, what combing and clawing,
what trickling and toying, and all to tawe out
money, you may be sure. And when they
come to washing—oh, how gingerly they be-
have themselves therein ! For then shall your
mouth be bossed with the lather or foam that
riseth of the balls (for they have their sweet
balls wherewith they use to wash), your eyes
closed must be anointed therewith also. Then
snap go the fingers full bravely, God wot. Thus
this tragedy ended, comes the warm clothes
to wipe and dry him withall ; next the ears
must be picked, and closed together again,

artificially, forsooth! The hair of the nostrils cut away, and everything done in order, comely to behold. The last action in the tragedy is the payment of money ; and lest these cunning barbers might seem unconscionable in asking much for their pains, they are of such a shameful modesty as they will ask nothing at all, but, standing to the courtesy and liberality of the giver, they will receive all that comes, how much soever it be, not giving any again, I warrant you ; for take a barber with that fault, and strike off his head. No, no ; such fellows are rarae aves in terris, nigrisque simillimæ cygnis—rare birds on the earth, and as scarce as black swans. You shall have also your fragrant waters for your face, wherewith you shall be all besprinkled ; your musick again, and pleasant harmony shall sound in your ears, and all to tickle the same with rare delight, and in the end your cloak shall be brushed, and 'God be with you, gentlemen !'"

John Gay issued in 1727 the first series of his "Fables," and in the one entitled "The Goat Without a Beard" we get a description of the barber's shop of the period :—

> " His pole, with pewter basins hung,
> .Black, rotten teeth in order strung,
> Rang'd cups that in the window stood,
> Lin'd with red rags, to look like blood,
> Did well his threefold trade explain,
> Who shav'd, drew teeth, and breath'd a vein."

The wooden chair is next referred to, and then it is stated :—

> "Mouth, nose, and cheeks, the lather hides :
> Light, smooth, and swift, the razor glides."

Old barbers' shops had their regulations in poetry and prose. Forfeits used to be enforced for breaches of conduct as laid down in laws which were exhibited in a conspicuous manner, and might be read while the customer was awaiting his turn for attention at the hands of the knight of the razor. Forfeits had to be paid for such offences as the following :—

> For handling the razors,
> For talking of cutting throats,
> For calling hair-powder flour,
> For meddling with anything on the shop-board.

Shakespeare alludes to this custom in "Measure for Measure," Act v. sc. 1, as follows :—

> "The strong statutes
> Stand like the forfeits in a barber's shop,
> As much in mock as mark."

Half a century ago there was hanging a code of laws in a barber's shop in Stratford-on-Avon, which the possessor mounted when he was an apprentice some fifty years previously. His master was in business as a barber at the time of the Garrick Jubilee in 1769, and he asserted that the list of forfeits was generally acknowledged by all the fraternity to have been in use for centuries. The following lines have found their way into several works, including Ingledew's "Ballads and Songs of Yorkshire" (1860). In some collections the lines are headed "Rules for

William Shakespeare (the Stratford Portrait).

Seemly Behaviour," and in others "The Barber of Thirsk's Forfeits." We draw upon Dr Ingledew for the following version, which is the best we have seen :—

"First come, first served—then come not late,
   And when arrived keep your sate ;

For he who from these rules shall swerve
Shall pay his forfeit—so observe.

" Who enters here with boots and spurs
Must keep his nook, for if he stirs
And gives with arm'd heel a kick,
A pint he pays for every prick.

" Who rudely takes another's turn
By forfeit glass—may manners learn ;
Who reverentless shall swear or curse
Must beg seven ha'pence from his purse.

" Who checks the barber in his tale,
Shall pay for that a gill of yale ;
Who will or cannot miss his hat
Whilst trimming pays a pint for that.

" And he who can but will not pay
Shall hence be sent half-trimmed away ;
For will he—nill he—if in fault,
He forfeit must in meal or malt.

" But mark, the man who is in drink
Must the cannikin, oh, never, never clink."

The foregoing table of forfeits was published
by Dr Kenrick in his review of Dr Johnson's
edition of Shakespeare in 1765, and it was
stated that he had read them many years before
in a Yorkshire town. This matter has been dis-
cussed at some length in *Notes and Queries*, and
it is asserted that the foregoing is a forgery.
Some interesting comments on the controversy
appeared in the issue of March 20th, 1869.

Women barbers in the olden time were by no

means uncommon in this country, and numerous accounts are given of the skilful manner they handled the razor. When railways were unknown and travellers went by stage-coach it took a considerable time to get from one important town to another, and shaving operations were often performed during the journey, and were usually done by women. In the byways of history we meet with allusions to "the five women barbers who lived in Drury-lane," who are said to have shamefully maltreated a woman in the days of Charles II. According to Aubrey, the Duchess of Albemarle was one of them.

At the commencement of the nineteenth century a street near the Strand was the haunt of black women who shaved with ease and dexterity. In St Giles'-in-the-Fields was another female shaver, and yet another woman wielder of the razor is mentioned in the "Topography of London," by J. T. Smith. "On one occasion," writes Smith, "that I might indulge the humour of being shaved by a woman, I repaired to the Seven Dials, where in Great St Andrew's Street a female performed the operations, whilst her husband, a strapping soldier in the Horse Guards, sat smoking his pipe." He mentions another woman barber in Swallow Street.

Two men from Hull some time ago went by an early morning trip to Scarborough, and getting up rather late the use of the razor was postponed until they arrived at the watering-place. Shortly after leaving the station they entered a barber's shop. A woman lathered their faces, which operation, although skilfully performed, caused surprise and gave rise to laughter. They fully expected a man would soon appear to complete the work, but they were mistaken. The female took a piece of brown paper from a shelf, and with this she held with her left hand the customer's nose, and in an artistic manner shaved him with her right hand. Some amusement was experienced, but the operation was finished without an accident. The gentlemen often told the story of their shave at Scarborough by a woman barber.

At Barnard Castle a wife frequently shaved the customers at the shop kept by her husband, who was often drunk and incapable of doing his work. Louth (Lincolnshire) boasted a female barber, who is said to have shaved lightly and neatly, and much better than most men.

Many stories, which are more or less true, are related respecting barbers. The following is said to be authentic, and we give it as related to us. The Duke of C—— upon one occasion entered a small barber's shop in Barnard Castle, and upon inquiring for the master was answered by an apprentice of fourteen that he was not at home. "Can you shave, then?" asked the duke. "Yes, sir, I always do," was the reply. "But can you shave without cutting?" "Yes, sir, I'll try," answered the youth. "Very well," said the

duke, while seating himself, and loading his
pistol ; "but look here, if you let any blood, as
true as I sit here I'll blow your brains out !
Now consider well before you begin." After a
moment's reflection, the boy began to make
ready, and said, "I'm not afraid of cutting
you, sir," and in a short time had completed
the feat without a scratch, to the complete satisfaction of the duke. In gentle tones his grace
asked, "Were you not afraid of having your
brains blown out, when you might have cut me
so easily ? "

"No, sir, not at all ; because I thought that
as soon as I should happen to let any blood,
before you could have time to fire I would cut
your throat."

The smart reply won from the duke a handsome reward. It need scarcely to be added
he never resumed his dangerous threats in a
barber's shop. A lesson was taught him for
life.

The barber of an English king boasted, says
a story, that he must be the most loyal man
in the realm, as he had every day the regal
throat at his mercy. The king was startled at
the observation, and concluded that the barbarous
idea could never have entered an honest head,
and for the future he resolved to grow a beard
as a precautionary measure against summary
execution.

With a barber's shop in Lichfield is associated

an amusing story, in which the chief figure was Farquhar, a dramatist, who attained a measure of success in the eighteenth century. His manner was somewhat pompous, and he resented with a great show of indignation the dalliance of the master of the shop. Whilst he was fuming, a little deformed man came up to him and performed the operation satisfactorily. The same day Farquhar was dining at the table of Sir Theophilus Biddulph, when he noticed the dwarf there. Taking the opportunity of following his host out of the room, he asked for an explanation of his conduct, and said that he deemed it an insult to be seated in such inferior company. Amazed at the charge, Sir Theophilus assured the dramatist that every one of the guests was a gentleman, and that they were his particular friends. Farquhar was not satisfied. " I am certain," he said, " that the little humpbacked man who sat opposite me is a barber who shaved me this morning." The host returned to the room and related the story which he had just heard. " Ay, yes," replied the guest, who was a well-born gentleman, " I can make the matter clear. It was I who was in the barber's shop this morning, and as Farquhar seemed in such a hurry, and the barber was out, I shaved him."

The works of the old dramatists and other publications contain allusions to barbers' music. It was the practice, as we have said, when a custómer was waiting for his turn in a barber's shop to pass his time playing on the gittern. Dekker mentions a "barber's cittern for every serving-man to play upon." Writing in 1583, Stubbes alludes to music at the barber's shop. In the "Diary of Samuel Pepys" we read : " After supper my Lord called for the lieutenant's cittern, and with two candlesticks with money in them for symballs, we made barber's music, with which my lord was well pleased." " My Lord was easily satisfied," says a well-known con- tributor to *Punch*, " and in our day would pro- bably have enjoyed ' the horgans.' " We may rest assured that barber's music was of question- able melody.

SUNDAY SHAVING

N bygone England, the churchyard was a common place for holding fairs and the vending of merchandise, and it was also customary for barbers to shave their customers there. In 1422, by a particular prohibition of Richard Flemmyng, Bishop of Lincoln, the observance of the custom was restrained.

The regulations of the Gild of Barber- Surgeons of York deal with Lord's Day observance. In 1592 a rule was made, ordering, under a fine of ten shillings, "that none of the barbers shall work or keep open their shop on Sunday, except two Sundays next or before the assize weeks." Another law on the question was made in 1676 as follows :—" This court, taking notice of several irregular and unreasonable practices committed by the Company of Barber-Surgeons within this city in shaving, trimming, and cutting of several strangers as well as citizens' hair and faces on the Lord's Day, which ought to be kept sacred, it is ordered by the whole consent of this court, and if any brother of the said Company shall at any time hereafter either by himself, servant, or substitute, tonse, barb, or trim any person on the Lord's Day, in any Inn or other public or private house or place, or shall go in or out of any such house or place on the said day with instruments used for that purpose, albeit the same cannot be positively proved, or made appear, but in case the Lord Mayor for the time being shall upon good circumstances consider and adjudge any such brother to have trimmed or barbed as is aforesaid, that then any such offender shall forfeit and pay for every such offence 10s., one half to the Lord Mayor, and the other to the use of the said Company, unless such brother shall voluntarily purge himself by oath to the contrary ; and the searchers of the said Company for the time being are to make diligent search

in all such as aforesaid public or private places
for discovery of such offenders."

The following abstract of an order of the
Barber-Surgeons of Chester shows that the
members of the Company were strict Sabba-
tarians :—

" 1680, seconde of July, ordered that no
member of the Company or his servant or
apprentice shall trim any person on the Lord's
Day commonly called Sunday."

In the Corporation records of Pontefract
under the year 1700 it is stated : "Whereas
divers complaints have been made that the
barbers of the said borough do frequently and
openly use and exercise their respective trades
upon the Lord's Day in profanation thereof, and
to the high displeasure of Almighty God. To
prevent such evil practices for the future it is
therefore ordered that no barber shall . . . use
or exercise the trade of a barber within the
borough of Pontefract upon the Lord's Day,
commonly called Sunday, nor shall trim or
shave any person upon that day, either publicly
or privately." We have in the last clause an
indication of public shaving performed in the
churchyard or the market place.

The churchwardens of Worksop parish,
Nottinghamshire, in 1729 paid half-a-crown
for a bond in which the barbers bound themselves "not to shave on Sundays in the
morning."

At a meeting of the barber-surgeons of
Newcastle-on-Tyne held in 1742 it was ordered
that no one should shave on a Sunday,
and that "no brother should shave John
Robinson till he pays what he owes to Robert
Shafto."

The operation was in bygone Scotland pronounced sinful if performed on a Sunday.
Members of congregations are entitled to object
to the settlement of ministers, says the Rev.
Dr Charles Rogers, provided they can substan-
tiate any charge affecting their life or doctrine.
Mr Davidson, presentee to Stenton in 1767,
and Mr Edward Johnstone, presentee to Moffat
in 1743, were objected to for desecrating the
Sabbath by shaving on that day. The settlement of Mr Johnstone was delayed four years,
so persistent were the objectors in maintaining
what they regarded as the proper observance of
the Sabbath.

The Rev. Patrick Brontë, father of the famous
novelists, was Perpetual Curate of Thornton in
Bradford Dale, from 1815 to 1820. Although
a sense of decency was sadly deficient among
the majority of the inhabitants of the district,
they kept watch on the clergy, and were ever
ready to make known to the world their presumed as well as their real offences and failings.
The mistakes of some of them are well illustrated
in an anecdote related by Mr Abraham Holroyd,
a well-known collector of local lore.   When Mr

Brontë resided at Thornton it was rumoured in the village that he had been seen by a Dissenter, through a chamber window, shaving himself on a Sunday morning, which was considered to be a very serious disregard of the obligation of Sabbath observance on the part of a clergyman. Mrs Ackroyd, a lady residing in the parish, had an interview with Mr Brontë on the subject. On his hearing what she had to say, he observed : " I should like you to keep what I say in your family ; but I never shaved myself in all my life, or was ever shaved by any one else. I have so little beard that a little clipping every three months is all that is necessary."

Occasionally, at the present day, barbers are brought before the magistrates for working on Sunday. They are summoned under an old Act of Charles II., for shaving on the Lord's Day. The maximum fine is five shillings, and the costs of a case cannot be recovered from the defendant. Generally the local hairdressers' association institutes the action.

FROM BARBER TO SURGEON

ROM the ancient but humble position of the barber is evolved the surgeon of modern times.   Perhaps some members of the medical profession would like to ignore the connection, but it is too true to be omitted from the pages of history.   The calling of a barber is of great antiquity.   We find in the Book of the Prophet Ezekiel (v. 1) allusions to the Jewish custom of the barber shaving the head as a sign of mourning.   In the remote past the art of surgery and the trade of barber were combined.   It is clear that in all parts of the civilised world, in bygone times, the barber acted as a kind of surgeon, or, to state his position more precisely, he practised phlebotomy, the dressing of wounds, etc.   Their shops were general in Greece about 420 B.C., and then, as now, were celebrated as places where the gossips met.   Barbers settled in Rome from Sicily in B.C. 299.

The clergy up to about the twelfth century had the care of men's bodies as well as their souls, and practised surgery and medicine. Barbers gained much experience from the monks, whom they assisted in surgical operations.   The practice of surgery involved the shedding of blood, and it was felt that this was incompatible with the functions of the clergy. After much consideration and discussion, in 1163, the Council of Tours, under Pope Alexander III., forbade the clergy to act as surgeons, but they were permitted to dispense medicine.

The Edict of Tours must have given satisfaction to the barbers, and they were not slow to avail themselves of the opportunities the change afforded them. In London, and it is to be feared in other places, the barbers advertised their blood-letting in a most objectionable manner. It was customary to put blood in their windows to attract the attention of the public. An ordinance was passed in 1307 directing the barbers in London to have the blood " privately carried into the Thames under the pain of paying two shillings to the use of the Sheriffs."

At an early period in London the barbers were banded together, and a gild was formed. In the first instance it seems that the chief object was the bringing together of the members at religious observances. They attended the funerals and obits of deceased members and their wives. Eventually it was transformed into a semi-social and religious gild, and subsequently became a trade gild. In 1308 Richard le Barber, the first master of the Barbers' Company, was sworn at the Guildhall, London. As time progressed the London Company of Barbers increased in importance.

In the first year of the reign of Edward IV. (1462) the barbers were incorporated by a Royal Charter, and it was confirmed by succeeding monarchs.

A change of title occurred in 1540, and it was then named the Company of Barber-Surgeons. Holbein painted a picture of Henry VIII. and the Barber-Surgeons. The painting is still preserved, and may be seen at the Barber-Surgeons' Hall, Monkwell Street, London. Pepys pronounces this " not a pleasant though a good picture." It is the largest and last work of Holbein.

The date assigned for its commencement was 1541, and it was completed after the death of the artist in 1543. It is painted on vertical oak boards, 5 ft. 11 in. high, and 10 ft. 2 in. long. It has been slightly altered since it was delivered to the Barber-Surgeons. The figures represent notable men belonging to the company and leaders of the healing art of the period at which it was painted.

In the reign of Henry VIII., not a few disputes occurred between the barbers and the surgeons. The following enactment was in force : " No person using any shaving or barbery in London shall occupy any surgery, letting of blood, or other matter, except of drawing teeth." Laws were made, but they could not, or at all events were not, enforced. The barbers acted often as surgeons, and the surgeons in-

Henry VIII. receiving the Barber-Surgeons.

creased their income by the use of the razor and shears. At this period, however, vigorous attempts were made to confine each to his legitimate work.

The Rev. J. L. Saywell has a note on bleeding in his " History and Annals of Northallerton " (1885). "Towards the early part of the nineteenth century," observes Mr Saywell, " a singular custom prevailed in the town and neighbourhood of Northallerton (Yorkshire). In the spring of the year nearly all the robust male adults, and occasionally females, repaired to a surgeon to be bled — a process which they considered essentially conduced to vigorous health." The charge for this operation was one shilling.

Parliament was petitioned, in 1542, praying that surgeons might be exempt from bearing arms and serving on juries, and thus be enabled without hindrance to attend to their professional duties. The request was granted, and to the present time medical men enjoy the privileges granted so long ago.

In 1745, the surgeons and the barbers were separated by Act of Parliament. The barber-surgeons lingered for a long time, the last in London, named Middleditch, of Great Suffolk Street, Southwark, only dying in 1821. Mr John Timbs, the popular writer, left on record that he had a vivid recollection of Middleditch's dentistry.

Over the last resting-places of some barber-surgeons are curious epitaphs. At Tewkesbury Abbey one in form of an acrostic is as follows :—

"Here lyeth the body of Thomas Merrett, of Tewkesbury, Barber-chirurgeon, who departed this life the 22nd day of October 1699.

Though only Stone Salutes the reader's eye,
Here (in deep silence) precious dust doth lye,
Obscurely Sleeping in Death's mighty store,
Mingled with common earth till time's no more.
Against Death's Stubborne laws, who dares repine,
Since So much Merrett did his life resigne.

Murmurs and Tears are useless in the grave,
Else hee whole Vollies at his Tomb might have.
Rest in Peace; who like a faithful steward,
Repair'd the Church, the Poore and needy cur'd;
Eternall mansions do attend the Just,
To clothe with Immortality their dust,
Tainted (whilst under ground) with wormes and rust."

Under the shadow of the ancient church of Bakewell, Derbyshire, is a stone containing a long inscription to the memory of John Dale, barber-surgeon, and his two wives, Elizabeth Foljambe and Sarah Bloodworth. It ends thus :—

"Know posterity, that on the 8th of April, in the year of grace 1757, the rambling remains of the above John Dale were, in the 86th yeare of his pilgrimage, laid upon his two wives.

This thing in life might raise some jealousy,
Here all three lie together lovingly,
But from embraces here no pleasure flows,
Alike are here all human joys and woes;
Here Sarah's chiding John no longer hears,
And old John's rambling Sarah no more fears;
A period's come to all their toylsome lives
The good man's quiet; still are both his wives.'

BYGONE BEARDS

HE history of the beard presents many items of interest connected with our own and other countries. Its importance belongs more to the past than to the present, but even to-day its lore is of a curious character. We find in Leviticus xiii. 29, the earliest mention of our theme, where Moses gives directions for the treatment of a plague in the beard, and a little later he forbids the Israelites to " mar the corners " of it. David, himself bearded, tells us that Aaron possessed one going down to the skirts of his garments. In David's reign ambassadors were sent to the King of Ammon, who, treating them as spies, cut off half of each of their beards. We are told that they were greatly ashamed, and David sent out to meet them, saying, " Tarry at Jericho until your beards be grown, and then return." To shave off the beard was considered by the Jews as a mark of the deepest grief.

To turn to the annals of our own land, we find that the ancient Britons did not cultivate the beard. The Saxons wore the hair of the head long, and upon the upper lip, but the chin was clean shaven. Harold, in his progress towards the fateful field of Hastings, sent spies in advance to obtain an idea as to the strength

C

of the enemy. On their return they stated among other things that " the host did almost seem to be priests, because they had all their face and both their lips shaven," a statement borne out by the representations of the Norman soldiers in the Bayeux tapestry. It is recorded that when the haughty victors had divided the broad

Bayeux Tapestry.
The above picture, showing two soldiers of William the Conqueror's army, is taken from the celebrated Bayeux tapestry.

lands of England among themselves, and when the Englishmen had been made to feel that they were a subdued and broken nation, the conquered people still kept up the old fashion of growing their hair long, so that they might resemble as little as possible their cropped and shaven masters.

Julius II., who ascended the Papal throne in 1503, was the first Pope to allow his beard

to grow, "in order," as he said, "to inspire
the greater respect among the faithful." A
curious custom of the Middle Ages was that
of imbedding three hairs from the king's beard
in the wax of the seal, in order to give greater
solemnity to the document. Another instance
of the value placed on this adornment of nature
by some nations comes to us in the story of
the Eastern potentate to whom the King of
England had sent a man without a beard as
his ambassador. The Eastern monarch flew
into a passion when the beardless visitor was
presented. " Had my master measured wisdom
by the beard," was the ready retort, " he would
have sent a goat."

It is said that beards came into fashion in
England in the thirteenth century, but by the nineteenth century they seem to have been given up by
those holding leading positions in the land. Traces
of beards do not appear on monumental brasses.
A revival of the practice of wearing the beard
occurred in the reign of Henry VIII., and in
some quarters attempts were made to repress
it. The authorities at Lincoln's Inn prohibited
lawyers wearing beards from sitting at the great
table, unless they paid double commons ; but
it is highly probable that this was before 1535,
when the king ordered his courtiers to "poll
their hair," and permit the crisp beard to grow.
Taxing beards followed, and the amount was
graduated according to the condition of the

person wearing this hirsute adornment. An
entry has often been reproduced from the
Burghmote Book of Canterbury, made in the
second year of the reign of Edward VI., to
the effect that the Sheriff of Canterbury and
another paid their dues for wearing beards, 3s.
4d. and 1s 8d. During the next reign, Queen
Mary does not appear to have meddled with
the beard. She sent four agents to Moscow,
and all were bearded ; one of the number, George
Killingworth, had an unusually long one, measure-
ing 5ft. 2in. in length, the sight of which caused
a smile to light up the face of Ivan the Terrible.
It is described as a thick, broad, and yellow
beard, and we are told that Ivan played with
it after dinner as if it were a new toy. When
Sir Thomas More laid his head on the block
he carefully put his beard aside, saying, " It
hath done no treason." John Knox (born 1505
and died 1572), the famous Scottish reformer,
whose name figures so largely in the religious
annals of his country, was remarkable for the
length of his beard. The Rev. John More was
a native of Yorkshire, and after being educated
at Cambridge settled at Norwich. He was one
of the worthiest clergymen in the reign of Queen
Elizabeth, and gained the name of " the Apostle
of Norwich." His beard was the largest and
longest of any Englishman of his time. He
used to give as his reason for wearing his beard
of unusual size " that no act of his life might

be unworthy of the gravity of his appearance."
He died at Norwich in 1592.

In the first year of the reign of Queen
Elizabeth an attempt was made to add to the

John Knox, born 1505, died 1572.

revenue by taxing at the rate of 3s. 4d. every
beard of above a fortnight's growth. It was an
abortive measure, and was not taken seriously. It
was never enforced, and people laughed at the
Legislature for attempting to raise money by
means of the beard. In Elizabeth's reign it was
considered a mark of fashion to dye the beard and

to cut it into a variety of shapes. In the reigns of the first James and the first Charles these forms

attracted not a little attention from the poets of the period. The rugged lines of Taylor, "the Water Poet," are among the best known, and if not of great poetical merit, they show considerable descriptive skill, John Taylor, the and enable us to realise the Water Poet, born fashions of his day. In his 1580, died 1654. "Superbiæ Flagellum," he describes a great variety of beards in his time, but omitted his own, which is that of a screw :—

" Now a few lines to paper I will put,
Of men's beards strange, and variable cut,
In which there's some that take as vain a pride
As almost in all other things beside ;
Some are reap'd most substantial like a brush,
Which makes a nat'rel wit known by the bush ;
And in my time of some men I have heard,
Whose wisdom have been only wealth and Beard ;
Many of these the proverb well doth fit,
Which says, bush natural, more hair than wit :
Some seem, as they were starched stiff and fine,
Like to the bristles of some angry swine ;
And some to set their love's desire on edge,
Are cut and prun'd like a quickset hedge ;
Some like a spade, some like a fork, some square,
Some round, some mow'd like stubble, some stark bare ;
Some sharp, stiletto fashion, dagger-like,
That may with whisp'ring, a man's eyes outpike ;
Some with the hammer cut, or roman T,
Their Beards extravagant, reform'd must be ;

The Lord Mayor of York escorting Princess Margaret through
York in 1503.   Shows the Beard of the Lord Mayor.

Some with the quadrate, some triangle fashion,
Some circular, some oval in translation ;
Some perpendicular in longitude ;
Some like a thicket for their crassitude ;
That heights, depths, breadths, triform, square, oval, round,
And rules geometrical in Beards are found."

Some curious lines appear in " Satirical Songs and Poems on Costume," edited by Frederick W. Fairholt, F.S.A., printed for the Percy Society, 1849. The piece which is entitled " The Ballad of the Beard," is reprinted from a collection of poems, entitled " Le Prince d'Amour," 1660, but it is evidently a production of the time of Charles I., if not earlier. " The varied form of the beard," says Fairholt, " which characterised the profession of each wearer, is amusingly descanted on, and is a curious fact in the chronicle of male fashions, during the first half of the seventeenth century." Taylor, the Water Poet, has alluded to the custom at some length ; and other writers of the day have so frequently mentioned the same thing, as to furnish materials for a curious (privately-printed) pamphlet, by J. A. Repton, F.S.A., on the various forms of the beard and mustachio. The beard, like " the Roman T," mentioned in the following ballad, is exhibited in our cut—Fig. 1—from a portrait of G. Raigersperg, 1649, in Mr Repton's book.

The stiletto-beard, as worn by Sir Edward

Coke, is seen in Fig. 2.   The needle-beard was narrower and more pointed.   The soldier's, or spade-beard, Fig. 3, is from a Dutch portrait, also in Mr Repton's book.   The stubble, or close-cropped beard of a judge, requires no pictorial illustration.   The bishop's-beard, Fig. 4, is given in Randle Holme's " Heraldry."   He calls it "the broad, or cathedral-beard, because

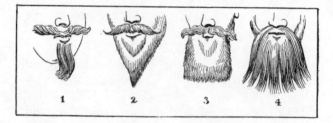

bishops, and grave men of the church, anciently did wear such beards."   "The beard of King Harry may be seen in any portrait of Henry VIII. and the amusing accuracy of the description tested.   The clown's beard, busy and not subject to any fashionable trimming, is sufficiently described in the words of the song."   We quote nearly the whole of this old ballad, in fact all that has a real bearing on the subject of the beard :—

"The beard, thick or thin, on the lip or chin,
    Doth dwell so near the tongue,
That her silence on the beard's defence
    May do her neighbour wrong.

Now a beard is a thing that commands in a king,
    Be his sceptres ne'er so fair :
Where the beard bears the sway, the people obey,
    And are subject to a hair.

'Tis a princely sight, and a grave delight,
    That adorns both young and old ;
A well thatcht face is a comely grace,
    And a shelter from the cold.

When the piercing north comes thundering forth,
    Let barren face beware ;
For a trick it will find, with a razor of wind,
    To shave the face that's bare.

But there's many a nice and strange device,
    That doth the beard disgrace ;
But he that is in such a foolish sin,
    Is a traitor to his face.

Now the beards there be of such a company,
    And fashions such a throng,
That it is very hard to handle a beard,
    Tho' it never be so long.

The Roman T, in its bravery,
    Doth first itself disclose,
But so high it turns, that oft it burns
    With the flames of a too red nose.

The stiletto-beard, oh ! it makes me afeared,
    It is so sharp beneath,
For he that doth place a dagger in's face,
    What wears he in his sheath ?

But, methinks, I do itch to go thro' stich
    The needle-beard to amend,
Which, without any wrong, I may call too long,
    For man can see no end.

The soldier's-beard doth march in shear'd
  In figure like a spade,
With which he'll make his enemies quake,
  And think their graves are made.

The grim stubble eke on the judge's chin,
  Shall not my verse despise ;
It is more fit for a nutmeg, but yet
  It grates poor prisoners' eyes.

What doth invest a bishop's breast
  But a milk-white spreading hair ?
Which an emblem may be of integrity,
  Which doth inhabit there.

But, oh ! let us tarry for the beard of King Harry,
  That grows about the chin,
With his bushy pride, and a grove on each side,
  And a champion ground between.

Last, the clown doth rush, with his beard like a bush,
  Which may be well endur'd."

Charles I. wore the Vandyke-beard, made familiar to us by the great artist. This fashion, set by the king, was followed by nearly the whole of his Cavaliers. It has been thought by some students of this subject that with the tragic death of the king the beard disappeared, but if we are to put our faith in an old song, dated 1660, we must conclude that with the Restoration it once more came into fashion. It says :—

  " Now of beards there be such company,
    Of fashions such a throng,
    That it is very hard to treat of the beard,
      Tho' it be never so long."

The Gunpowder Conspirators, from a print published immediately after the discovery. Shows the Beards in Fashion in 1605.

It did not remain popular for any length of time, the razor everywhere keeping down its growth.

Sir Walter Scott's great grandsire was called "Beardie." He was an ardent Jacobite, and made a vow that he would never shave his beard until the Stuarts were restored. "It would have been well," said the novelist, "if his zeal for the vanished dynasty had stopped with letting his beard grow. But he took arms and intrigued in their cause, until he lost all he had in the world, and, as I have heard, ran a narrow risk of being hanged, had it not been for the interference of Anne, Duchess of Buccleuch and Monmouth." Sir Walter refers to him in the introduction to Canto VI. of "Marmion":—

> "With amber beard and flaxen hair,
>   And reverend apostolic air.
>   Small thought was his, in after time
>   E'er to be pitched into a rhyme.
>   The simple sire could only boast
>   That he was loyal to his cost ;
>   The banish'd race of kings revered,
>   And lost his land—but kept his beard."

He died in 1729 at Kelso. "Beardie's" second son, named Robert, was a farmer at Sandyknowe, and was Sir Walter Scott's grandfather.

A contributor to *Notes and Queries*, for October 1st, 1859, gives the following interesting particulars of a Shaving Statute relating to Ireland :—"In a parliament held at Trim by John Talbot, Earl of Shrewsbury, then Lord-

Lieutenant, anno 1447, 25 Henry VI., it was enacted 'That every Irishman must keep his upper lip shaved, or else be used as an Irish enemy.' The Irish at this time were much attached to the national foppery of wearing mustachios, the fashion then throughout Europe, and for more than two centuries after. The unfortunate Paddy who became an enemy for his beard, like an enemy was treated ; for the treason could only be pardoned by the surrender of his land. Thus two benefits accrued to the king: his enemies were diminished, and his followers provided for ; many of whose descendants enjoy the confiscated properties to this day, which may appropriately be designated Hair-breadth estates." The effects of this statute became so alarming that the people submitted to the English revolutionary razor, and found it more convenient to resign their beards than their lands. This agrarian law was repealed by Charles I., after existing two hundred years.

The Macedonian soldiers were ordered by Alexander to shave, lest their beards should be handles for the enemy to capture them by. The smooth chin was adopted in the Greek army. To pull a person's beard has from remote times been regarded as an act of most degrading insult. Dr Doran tells a tragic story bearing on this usage. "When the Jew," says the doctor, "who hated and feared the living Cid Rui Dios, heard that the great Spaniard was dead, he contrived to get into the room where the body lay, and he indulged his revengeful spirit by contemptuously plucking at the beard. But the 'son of somebody' (the hidalgo) was plucked temporarily into life and indignation by the outrage ; and starting up, endeavoured to get his sword, an attempt which killed the Jew by mere fright which it caused." In Afghanistan "the system of administering justice was such," says the "Life of Abdur Rahman" (London, 1890) "that the humble were able to bring their claims before the sovereign by the simple process of getting hold of the sovereign's beard and turban, which meant to throw one's complaints on the shame of his beard, to which he was bound to listen. One day I was going to the Hum-hum (Turkish bath) when a man and his wife, running fast, rushed into the bathroom after me, and the husband, having got hold of my beard from the front, the wife was pulling me at the same time from behind. It was very painful, as he was pulling my beard rather hard. As there was no guard or sentry near to deliver me from their hands, I begged them to leave my beard alone, saying that I could listen without my beard being pulled, but all in vain. I was rather sorry that I had not adopted the fashion of the Europeans, whose faces are clean shaven. I ordered that in future a strong guard should be placed at the door of the Hum-hum."

Some of the ancient faiths regarded the beard as an appendage not to be touched with the razor, and a modern instance bearing on the old belief will be read with interest. Mr Edward Vizetelly, in his entertaining volume "From Cyprus to Zanzibar" (London, 1901), tells some good stories about the priests in Cyprus. Mr Vizetelly went to the island as soon as it passed into the hands of the British Government, and remained there a few years. "On one occasion," he says, "when I happened to be in the bazaar at Larnaca in the early afternoon, I was amazed to witness all the shopkeepers, apart from the Maltese, suddenly putting up their shutters, as if panic-stricken, but without any apparent cause. Inquiring the reason, it was only vouchsafed to me that some-one had shaved off a priest's beard." The priest had been imprisoned for felling a tree in his own garden, which was against the laws of the land then in force. When in gaol the recalcitrant priest had his unclean hair and beard shorn off, in accordance with the prison regulations. The authorities were not aware that the hirsute adornments of the Orthodox Catholic faith were sacred. The act roused the Cyprist ire, and the High Commissioner had to issue orders that if any priest was locked up in future his hair and beard were to be left alone.

Respecting the beard are some popular sayings, and we deal with a few as follows.

A familiar example is "To pull the devil by the beard." When Archbishop Laud was advised to escape from this country he said, "If I should get into Holland, I should expose myself to the insults of those sectaries there, to whom my character is odious, and have every Anabaptist come to pull me by the beard." This insulting saying is by no means confined to England. To demand a person's beard was regarded as a still greater insult. King Ryons, when he sent a messenger to King Arthur to demand his beard, received the following answer :—

"Wel, sayd Arthur, thou hast said thy message, yᵉ whiche is yᵉ most vylaynous and lewdest message that ever man herd sent unto a kynge. Also thou mayst see, my berd is ful yong yet to make a purfyl of hit. But telle thou thy kynge this, I owe hym none homage, ne none of myn elders, but, or it be longe to, he shall do me homage on bothe his kneys, or else he shall lese his hede by yᵉ feith of my body, for this is yᵉ most shamefullest message that ever I herd speke of. I have aspyed, thy kyng met never yet with worshipful men ; but tell hym, I wyll have his hede without he doo me homage. Thenne yᵉ messager departed." ("The Byrth, Lyf and Actes of Kyng Arthur," edit. by Caxton, 1485, reprinted 1817.)

"To make any one's beard" is an old saying, which means "to cheat him," or "to deceive him." We read in Chaucer's *Prologue to the Wife of Bath* thus :—

> "In faith he shal not kepe me, but me lest :
> Yet coude I make his berd, so mete I the."

Geoffrey Chaucer, born about 1340, died 1400.

And again, in the "Reve's Tale," the Miller said :—

> "I trow, the clerkes were aferde
> Yet can a miller make a clerkes bearde,
> For all his art."

A more familiar saying is "To beard a person," meaning to affront him, or to set him at defiance.

Todd explains the allusion in a note in his edition of Spenser's *Faerie Queene*—"did beard affront him to his face"; so Shakespeare's *King Henry IV.*, Part I. Act i.: "I beard thee to thy face"—Fr. "Faire la Barbe a quelqu'un." Ital. "Fa la barbe ad uno" (Upton.)

See Steevens's note on the use of the word Beard in *King Henry IV.*, which is adopted, he says, "from romances, and originally signified to 'cut off the beard.'" Mr John Ady Repton, F.S.A., to whom we are mainly indebted for our illustrations of these popular sayings, directs attention to a specimen of defiance expressed in Agamemnon's speech to Achilles, as translated by Chapman :—

> ——" and so tell thy strength how eminent
> My power is, being compared with thine :
>   all other making feare
> To vaunt equality with me, or in this
>   proud kind beare
> Their beards against me."

In Shirley's play, *A Contention for Honour and Riches*, 1633 :—

> "You have worn a sword thus long to show ye hilt,
> Now let the blade appear.
> COURTIER.—Good Captain Voice,
> It shall, and teach you manners ; I have yet
> No ague, I can look upon your buff,
> And punto beard, and call for no strong waters."

"It is difficult to ascertain," says Repton, "when the custom of pulling the nose superseded

that of pulling the beard, but most probably
when the chin became naked and close shaven,
affording no longer a handle for insult." In the
reign of James II., William Cavendish, Earl of
Devonshire, paid £30,000 for offering this insult
to a person at Court. An earlier instance of
pulling the nose may be found in Ben Jonson's
Epicœne, or the Silent Woman, Act iv. sc. 5.

In " Aubrey's Letters " is an allusion to wiping
the beard. " Ralph Kettle, D.D.," we read,
" preached in St Mary's Church at Oxford, and,
in conclusion of a sermon, said, ' But now I see
it is time for me to shutt up my booke, for I see
the doctors' men come in wiping their beards
from the ale-house (he could from the pulpit
plainly see them, and 't was their custome to go
there, and, about the end of the Sermon, to
return to wayte on their masters)." An old play
by Lyly, entitled *Mother Bombie* (1597-98), Act i.
sc. 3, contains the following passage :—

" Tush, spit not you, and I'll warrant I, my
beard is as good as a handkerchief."

Our quotations from old plays are mainly
drawn from Repton's little book, " Some account
of the Beard and Moustachio," of which one
hundred copies were printed for private circula-
tion in 1839.

The extracts which we have reproduced are
not such as to cause the beard to find favour
with the ladies. In Marston's *Antonio and Melida*,
(1602), Act v., we read as follows :—

"PIERO.—Faith, mad niece, I wonder when thou wilt marry?

"ROSSALINE.—Faith, kind Uncle, when men abandon jealousy, forsake taking tobacco, and cease to wear their beards so rudely long. Oh! to have a husband with a mouth continually smoking, with a bush of furze on the ridge of his chin, ready still to flop into his foaming chaps; ah! 't is more than most intolerable."

In another part of the same play are other objections to the mustachios. We find in other old plays allusions to women combing and stroking beards. "There is no accounting," says Repton, "for the taste of ladies. Charles Brandon, Duke of Suffolk, with his large massive beard, won the heart of the fair sister of Henry VIII. Although the 'Cloth of friez may not be too bold,' the courtship was most probably begun by the lady (*i.e.* the Cloth of Gold). Although ladies do not speak out, they have a way of expressing their wishes by the 'eloquence of eyes.' That the fair princess ever amused herself in combing or brushing her husband's beard is not recorded in the history of England." Many references find a place in bygone plays relating to combs and brushes for the beard.

Starching the beard was an operation which occupied some time if carefully performed. It is stated in the "Life of Mrs Elizabeth Thomas," published in 1731, of Mr Richard Shute, her grandfather, a Turkey merchant, that he was very nice in the mode of that age, his valet being some hours every morning in starching his beard, and curling his whiskers, during which time a gentleman, whom he maintained as a companion, always read to him upon some useful subject. In closing, we have to state that cardboard boxes were worn at night in bed to protect the beard from being disarranged.

TAXING THE BEARD

EARDS, in some instances, were taxed in bygone England, but not to the same extent as in Russia, which had numerous singular laws in force for nearly sixty years. In nearly all parts of Europe, by the commencement of the eighteenth century, the custom of wearing beards had been given up. Peter the Great was wishful that his subjects should conform to the prevailing fashion. In 1705 he imposed a tax upon all those who wore either a beard or a moustache, varying from thirty to one hundred roubles per annum. It was fixed according to the rank of the taxpayer. A peasant, for instance, was only required to pay two dengops, equal to one copeck, whenever he passed through the gate of a town. This tax gave rise to much discontent, and in enforcing it the utmost vigilance had to be exercised to prevent an outbreak in the country. Notwithstanding this, the law was, in 1714, put into operation in St Petersburg, which had previously been exempt. In 1722 it was ordered that all who retained their beards should wear a particular dress and pay fifty roubles annually. If a man would not shave, and was unable to pay, he was sentenced to hard labour. This law was extended to the provinces, but in 1723 peasants bringing produce into towns were wholly relieved from this tax. Peter passed away in 1725, and Catherine I. confirmed all the edicts relating to the beard in the ukase dated 4th August 1726.

A decree was issued by Peter II. in 1728 permitting peasants employed in agriculture to wear their beards. Fifty roubles had to be paid by all other persons, and the tax was rigidly enforced. The Empress Anne took a firm attitude against the beard. In 1731 she promulgated a ukase by which all persons not engaged in husbandry retaining their beards were entered in the class of Raskolnicks, in addition to paying the beard tax of fifty roubles, double the amount of all other taxes.

In 1743 the Empress Elizabeth confirmed the existing decrees in all their force. Peter III., on his accession to the throne in 1762, intended to strengthen the laws of his predecessors, and prepared some stringent measures; but his

sudden death prevented them from being put
into force. His widow, Catherine II. (1762),
did not share his feelings in this matter, and
immediately on obtaining sovereign power she
removed every restriction relating to the beard.
She invited the Raskolnicks, who had fled from
the country to avoid the objectionable edicts,
to return, and assigned land to them for their
settlement.

During thirty-eight years in Russia, the

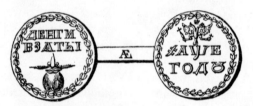

Russian Beard Token, A.D. 1705.

beard-token or Borodoráia (the bearded), as it
was called, was in use. As we write we have
one of these tokens before us, and on one side are
represented a nose, mouth, moustaches, and a
large flowing beard, with the inscription " dinge
vsatia," which means " money received " ; the re-
verse bears the year in, Russian characters
(equivalent to " 1705 year "), and the black eagle
of the empire.

Our facts are mainly drawn from a paper
by Mr Walter Hawkins in the " Numismatic
Chronicle," volume vii., 1845. He says that

beard-tokens are rare, and he thinks that the national aversion to their origin probably caused their destruction or dispersion after they had served their purpose for the year.

POWDERING THE HAIR

N the olden days hair-powder was largely used in this country, and many circumstances connected with its history are curious and interesting. We learn from Josephus that the Jews used hair-powder, and from the East it was no doubt imported into Rome. The history of the luxurious days of the later Roman Empire supplies some strange stories. At this period gold-dust was employed by several of the emperors. "The hair of Commodus," it is stated on the authority of Herodian, "glittered from its natural whiteness, and from the quantity of essences and gold-dust with which it was loaded, so that when the sun was shining it might have been thought that his head was on fire."

It is supposed, and not without a good show of reason, that the Saxons used coloured hair-powder, or perhaps they dyed their hair. In Saxon pictures the beard and hair are often painted blue. Strutt supplies interesting notes on the subject. " In some instances," he says, " which, indeed, are not so common, the hair is represented of a bright red colour, and in others it is of a green and orange hue. I have no doubt existing in my own mind, that arts of some kind were practised at this period to colour the hair ; but whether it was done by tingeing or dyeing it with liquids prepared for that purpose according to the ancient Eastern custom, or by powders of different hues cast into it, agreeably to the modern practice, I shall not presume to determine."

It was customary among the Gauls to wash the hair with a lixivium made of chalk in order to increase its redness. The same custom was maintained in England for a long period, and was not given up until after the reign of Elizabeth. The sandy-coloured hair of the queen greatly increased the popularity of the practice.

The satirists have many allusions to this subject, more especially those of the reigns of James and Charles I. In a series of epigrams entitled " Wit's Recreations," 1640, the following appears under the heading of *Our Monsieur Powder-wig* :—

> " Oh, doe but marke yon crisped sir, you meet !
> How like a pageant he doth walk the street !
> See how his perfumed head is powdered ore ;
> 'Twou'd stink else, for it wanted salt before."

In " Musarum Deliciæ," 1655, we read :—

> " At the devill's shopps you buy
> A dresse of powdered hayre,
> On which your feathers flaunt and fly ;
> But i'de wish you have a care,
> Lest Lucifer's selfe, who is not prouder,
> Do one day dresse up your haire with a powder."

From the pen of R. Younge, in 1656, appeared " The Impartial Monitor." The author closes with a tirade against female follies in these words : " It were a good deed to tell men also of mealing their heads and shoulders, of wearing fardingales about their legs, etc. ; for these likewise deserve the rod, since all that are discreet do but hate and scorn them for it." A *Loyal Litany* against the Oliverians runs thus :—

> " From a king-killing saint,
> Patch, powder, and paint,
> Libera nos, Domine."

Massinger, in the " City Madam," printed in 1679, describing the dress of a rich merchant's wife, mentions powder thus :—

> " Since your husband was knighted, as I said,
> The reverend hood cast off, your borrowed hair
> Powdered and curled, was by your dresser's art,
> Formed like a coronet, hanged with diamonds
> And richest orient pearls."

John Gay, in his poem, " Trivia, or the Art of Walking the Streets of London," published n 1716, advises in passing a coxcomb—

"Him like the Miller, pass with caution by,
Lest from his shoulder clouds of powder fly."

We learn from the "Annals of the Barber-Surgeons" some particulars respecting the taxing of powder. On 8th August 1751, "Mr John Brooks," it is stated, "attended and produced a deed to which he requested the subscription of the Court; this deed recited that by an Act of Parliament passed in the tenth year of Queen Anne, it was enacted that a duty of twopence per pound should be laid upon all starch imported, and of a penny per pound upon all starch made in Great Britain, that no perfumer, barber, or seller of hair-powder should mix any powder of alabaster, plaster of Paris, whiting, lime, etc. (sweet scents excepted), with any starch to be made use of for making hair-powder, under a pain of forfeiting the hair-powder and £50, and that any person who should expose the same for sale should forfeit it and £20." Other details were given in the deed, and the Barber-Surgeons gave it their support, and promised twenty guineas towards the cost of passing the Bill through Parliament.

A few years prior to the above proceeding we gather from the *Gentleman's Magazine* particulars of some convictions for using powder not made in accordance with the laws of the land. "On the 20th October, 1745," it is recorded, "fifty-one barbers were convicted before the commissioners of excise, and fined in the penalty of £20, for having in their custody hair-powder not made of starch, contrary to Act of Parliament : and on the 27th of the same month, forty-nine other barbers were convicted of the same offence, and fined in the like penalty."

Before powder was used, the hair was generally greased with pomade, and powdering operations were attended with some trouble. In houses of any pretension was a small room set apart for the purpose, and it was known as the powdering-room. Here were fixed two curtains, and the person went behind, exposing the head only, which received its proper supply of powder without any going on the clothes of the individual dressed. In the *Rambler*, No. 109, under date 1751, a young gentleman writes that his mother would rather follow him to his grave than see him sneak about with dirty shoes and blotted fingers, hair unpowdered, and a hat uncocked.

We have seen that hair-powder was taxed, and on the 5th of May, 1795, an Act of Parliament was passed taxing persons using it. Pitt was in power, and being sorely in need of money, hit upon the plan of a tax of a guinea per head on those who used hair powder. He was prepared to meet much ridicule by this movement, but he saw that it would yield a considerable revenue, estimating it at as much as £200,000 a year. Fox, with force, said that a fiscal arrangement dependent on a capricious fashion must be regarded as an absurdity, but the Opposition were unable to defeat the proposal, and the Act was passed. Pitt's powerful rival, Charles James Fox, in his early manhood, was one of the most fashionable men in London. Here are a few particulars of his "get up" about 1770, drawn from the *Monthly Magazine :* "He had his chapeau-bas, his red-heeled shoes, and his blue hair-powder." Later, when Pitt's tax was gathered, like other Whigs, he refused to use hair-powder. For more than a quarter of a century it had been customary for men to wear their hair long, tied in a pig-tail and powdered. Pitt's measure gave rise to a number of Crop Clubs. The *Times* for April 14th, 1795, contains particulars of one. "A numerous club," says the paragraph, "has been formed in Lambeth, called the Crop Club, every member of which, on his entrance, is obliged to have his head docked as close as the Duke of Bridgewater's old bay coach-horses. This assemblage is instituted for the purpose of opposing, or rather evading, the tax on powdered heads." Hair cropping was by no means confined to the humbler ranks of society. The *Times* of April 25th, 1795, reports that : "The following noblemen and gentlemen were at the party with the Duke of Bedford, at Woburn Abbey, when a general cropping and combing out of hair-powder took place : Lord W. Russell, Lord Villiers, Lord Paget, etc., etc. They entered into an engagement to forfeit a sum of money if any of them wore their hair tied, or powdered, within a certain period. Many noblemen and gentlemen in the county of Bedford have since followed the example : it has become general with the gentry in Hampshire, and the ladies have left off wearing powder." Hair powder did not long continue in use in the army, for in 1799 it was abolished on account of the high price of flour, caused through the bad harvests. Using flour for the hair instead of for food was an old grievance among the poor. In the "Art of Dressing the Hair," 1770, the author complains :—

> "Their hoarded grain contractors spare,
> And starve the poor to beautify the hair."

Pitt's estimates proved correct, for in the first year the tax produced £210,136. The tax was increased from a guinea to one pound three shillings and sixpence. Pitt's Tory friends gave him loyal support. The Whigs might taunt them by calling them "guinea-pigs," it mattered little, for they were not merely ready to pay the tax for themselves, but to pay patriotic guineas for their servants. A number of persons were exempt from paying the tax, including "the royal family and their servants, the clergy with an income of under £100 per annum, subalterns, non-commissioned officers and privates of the yeomanry and volunteers enrolled during the past year. A father having more than two

E

unmarried daughters might obtain on payment
for two, a licence for the remainder." A gentleman took out a licence for his butler, coachman,
and footman, etc., and if he changed during the
year it stood good for the newly engaged
servants.

Powder was not wholly set aside by ladies until
1793, when with consideration Queen Charlotte
abandoned its use, swayed no doubt by her
desire to cheapen, in that time of dearth, the
flour of which it was made. It has been said
its disuse was attributable to Sir Joshua Reynolds,
Angelica Kauffmann, and other painters of their
day, but it is much more likely that the artists
painted the hair " full and flowing " because they
found it so, not that they as a class dictated to
their patronesses in despite of fashion. The
French Revolution had somewhat to do with the
change ; a powdered head or wig was a token of
aristocracy, and as the fashion might lead to the
guillotine, sensible people discarded it long
before the English legislature put a tax upon its
use. With reference to this Sir Walter Scott
says, in the fifth chapter of " The Antiquary : "
" Regular were the Antiquary's inquiries at an
old-fashioned barber, who dressed the only three
wigs in the parish, which, in defiance of taxes
and times, were still subjected to the operation
of powdering and frizzling, and who for that
purpose divided his time among the three
employers whom fashion had yet left him.

"'Fly with this letter, Caxon,' said the senior ('The Antiquary'), holding out his missive, 'fly to Knockwinnock, and bring me back an answer. Go as fast as if the town council were met and waiting for the provost, and the provost was waiting for his new powdered wig.' 'Ah, sir,' answered the messenger, with a deep sigh, 'thae days hae lang gane by. Deil a wig has a provost of Fairport worn sin' auld Provost Jervie's time—and he had a quean of a servant lass that dressed it hersel', wi' the doup o' a candle and a dredging box. But I hae seen the day, Monkbarns, when the town council of Fairport wad hae as soon wanted their town-clerk, or their gill of brandy owerhead after the haddies, as they wad hae wanted ilk ane a weel-favoured, sonsy, decent periwig on his pow. Hegh, sirs! nae wonder the commons will be discontent, and rise against the law, when they see magistrates, and bailies, and deacons, and the provost himsel', wi' heads as bald an' as bare as one o' my blocks.'" It was not in Scotland alone that the barber was peripatetic. "In the eighteenth century," says Mrs G. Linnæus Banks, author of the "Manchester Man" and other popular novels, "he waited on his chief customers or patrons at their own homes, not merely to shave, but to powder the hair or the wig, and he had to start on his round betimes. Where the patron was the owner of a spare periwig it might be dressed in advance, and sent

home in a box or mounted on a stand, such as
a barrister keeps handy at the present day. But
when ladies had powdered top-knots, the hairdresser made his harvest, especially when a ball
or a rout made the calls for his services many
and imperative. When at least a couple of hours
were required for the arrangement of a single
toupée or tower, or commode, as the head-dress
was called, it may be well understood that for
two or three days prior to the ball the hairdresser was in demand, and as it was impossible
to lie down without disarranging the structure
he had raised on pads, or framework of wire,
plastering with pomatum and disguising with
powder, the belles so adorned or disfigured were
compelled to sit up night and day, catching
what sleep was possible in a chair. And when
I add that a head so dressed was rarely dis-
turbed for ten days or a fortnight, it needs no
stretch of imagination to realise what a mass of
loathsome nastiness the fine ladies of the last
century carried about with them, or what strong
stomachs the barbers must have had to deal
with them."

When the eighteenth century was drawing to
a close the cry for bread was heard in the land.
In 1795 the price of grain rose very high on
account of the small supplies coming into the
market. Bakers in many instances sold bread
deficient in weight, and to check the fraud many
shopkeepers were fined sums from £64, 5s. to

£106, 5s. The Privy Council gave the matter serious consideration, and strongly urged that families should refrain from having puddings, pies, and other articles made of flour. King George III. gave orders in 1795 for the bread used in his household to be made of meal and rye mixed. He would not permit any other sort to be baked, and the Royal Family partook of the same quality of bread as was eaten by the servants.

A great deal of flour was used as hair powder, and an attempt was made to check its use. The following is a copy of a municipal proclamation issued at Great Yarmouth, the original of which is preserved in the office of the Town Clerk :—

"DISUSE OF HAIR POWDER.

"Owing to the present enormous price of corn, and the alarming approach of a scarcity in that most necessary article, many towns throughout the kingdom have set the laudable example of leaving off for a time the custom of wearing powder for the hair ; by which means a great quantity of wheat must infallibly be saved to the nation ; and if the price be not reduced, it may at least be prevented from increasing. We, therefore, the Mayor, Justices, and principal inhabitants of Great Yarmouth, do recommend this example as worthy to be imitated ; and we flatter ourselves the Military will not hesitate to adopt it, being fully convinced that appearances are at all times to be sacrificed to the public weal, and that in doing this they really do good.

"W. TAYLOR, Mayor.

"January 27th, 1795."

Lord Hawkesbury, on February 20th, 1800, presented a bill in the House of Commons prohibiting bakers from vending bread that had not been baked a certain number of hours. The bill was read a first and second time, and immediately went into Committee. It passed this stage, and went to the House of Lords, where it was at once passed. Subsequently it received the royal assent.

We find in a local paper, dated March 31st, 1800, that a baker in Hull was fined £10 for selling bread within twenty-four hours of its having heen been baked, agreeable to Act of Parliament for that purpose.

The Tories often regarded with mistrust any persons who did not use hair-powder. The Rev. J. Charles Cox, LL.D., F.S.A., the eminent antiquary, relates a good story respecting his grandfather. "So late as 1820," says Dr Cox, "Major Cox of Derby, an excellent Tory, declined for some time to allow his son Edward to become a pupil of a well-known clerical tutor, for the sole reason that the clergyman did not powder, and wore his hair short, arguing that he must therefore be a dangerous revolutionist."

In 1869 the tax on hair-powder was repealed, when only some 800 persons paid it, producing about £1000 per year.

THE AGE OF WIGS

AT the present time, when the wig is no longer worn by the leaders of fashion, we cannot fully realise the important place it held in bygone times. Professional as well as fashionable people did not dare to appear in public without their wigs, which vied with each other in size and style.

To trace the origin of the wig our investigations must be carried to far distant times. It was worn in Egypt in former days, and the Egyptians are said to have invented it, not merely as a covering for baldness, but as a means of adding to the attractiveness of the person wearing it. On the mummies of Egypt wigs are found, and we give a picture of one now in the British Museum. This particular wig probably belonged to a female, and was found near the small temple of Isis, Thebes. It was customary in Egypt to shave the head, and the wig was an excellent covering for the head, much better than a turban, for the wig protected it from

the rays of the sun, and its texture allowed the
transpiration of the head to escape. The wigs
were worn both within the house and out of
doors. The specimens of Egyptian wigs in the
British Museum consist of curled hair in the
upper portions, and the lower parts and sides

Egyptian Wig (probably for female), from the British Museum.

are made of plaited hair. Ointment was used
at the top of the wig in the same manner as if
it had been hair growing on the head.

Assyrian sculptures frequently represent the
wig, and its use is recorded among ancient
nations including Persians, Medes, Lydians,
Carians, Greeks, and Romans. *Galerus*, a round
cap, was the common name among the Romans
for a wig.

The early fathers of the Church denounced the wig as an invention of the Evil One. St Gregory of Nazianzus, as a proof of the virtue of his simple sister Gorgonia, said " she neither cared to curl her own hair, nor to repair its lack of beauty by the aid of a wig." St Jerome pronounced these adornments as unworthy of Christianity. The matter received consideration, or perhaps, to put it more correctly, condemnation, at many councils, commencing at Constantinople, and coming down to the Provincial Council at Tours. The wig was not tolerated, even if worn as a joke. " There is no joke in the matter," said the enraged St Bernard : "the woman who wears a wig commits a mortal sin." St John Chrysostom pleaded powerfully against this enormity ; and others might be mentioned who spoke with no uncertain sound against this fashion.

Dr Doran relates a strange story, saying that St Jerome vouches for its authenticity, and that by him it was told to deter ladies from wearing wigs. " Prætexta," to use Doran's words, " was a very respectable lady, married to a somewhat paganist husband, Hymetius. Their niece, Eustachia, resided with them. At the instigation of the husband, Prætexta took the shy Eustachia in hand, attired her in a splendid dress and covered her fair neck with ringlets. Having enjoyed the sight of the modest maiden so attired, Prætexta went to bed. To that bedside immediately descended an angel, with wrath upon his brow, and billows of angry sounds rolling from his lips. ' Thou hast,' said the spirit, ' obeyed thy husband rather than the Lord, and hast dared to deck the hair of a virgin, and make her look like a daughter of earth. For this do I wither up thy hands, and bid them recognise the enormity of thy crime in the amount of thy anguish and bodily suffering. Five months more shalt thou live, and then Hell shall be thy portion ; and if thou art bold enough to touch the head of Eustachia again, thy husband and thy children shall die even before thee.' "

Church history furnishes some strange stories against wearing wigs, and the following may be taken as a good example. Clemens of Alexandria, so runs the tale, surprised wig-wearers by telling those who knelt at church that to receive the blessing, they must please to bear in mind that the benediction remained on the wig, and did not pass through to the wearer ! Some immediately removed their wigs, but others allowed them to remain, no doubt hoping to receive a blessing.

History supplies many interesting passages bearing on our present investigations. The Lycians, having been engaged in war, were defeated. Mausoleus, their conqueror, ruthlessly directed the subdued men to have their heads shaven. This was humiliating in the extreme, and the Lycians were keenly alive to their ridiculous appearance. The king's general was tempted with bribes, and finally yielded, and allowed wigs to be imported for them from Greece, and thus the symbol of degradation became the pink of Lycian fashion.

Hannibal, the brave soldier, is recorded to have worn two sorts of wigs, one to improve, and the other to disguise his person.

Wigs are said to have been worn in England in the reign of King Stephen, but their palmy days belong to the seventeenth and the earlier part of the eighteenth centuries. According to Stow, they were introduced into this country about the time of the Massacre of Paris, but they are not often alluded to until the reign of Queen Elizabeth. The earliest payment for one in the Privy Purse expenses occurs in December 1529, and is for twenty shillings "for a perwyke for Sexton, the king's fool." Some twenty years later wigs, or, to give the full title, periwigs, became popular. In France the mania was at its height in the reign of Louis XIV. We are told that in 1656 he had not fewer than forty court perruquiers, and these, by an Order of Council, were declared artistes. In addition to this, Le Gros instituted at Paris an Académie de France des Perruquiers. Robinson records that a storm was gathering about their heads. He tells us " the celebrated Colbert, amazed at the large sums spent for foreign hair, conceived the idea of prohibiting the wearing of wigs at Court, and tried to introduce a kind of cap." He lost the day, for it was proved that more money reached the country for wigs than went out to purchase hair. The fashion increased; larger wigs were worn, and some even cost £200 apiece.

Charles II. was the earliest English king represented on the Great Seal wearing a large periwig. Dr Doran assures us that the king did not bring the fashion to Whitehall. "He forbade," we are told, "the members of the Universities to wear periwigs, smoke tobacco, or to read their sermons. The members did all three, and Charles soon found himself doing the first two."

Pepys' "Diary" contains much interesting information concerning wigs. Under date of 2nd November, 1663, he writes: "I heard the Duke say that he was going to wear a periwig, and says the King also will. I never till this day observed that the King is mighty gray." It was perhaps the change in the colour of his Majesty's hair that induced him to assume the head-dress he had previously so strongly condemned.

As might be expected, Pepys, who delighted to be in the fashion, adopted the wig. He took time to consider the matter, and had consultations with Mr Jervas, his old barber, about the affair. Referring in his "Diary" to one of his visits to his hairdresser, Pepys says, "I did try

two or three borders and periwigs, meaning to
wear one, and yet I have no stomach for it ;
but that the pains of keeping my hair clean is
great. He trimmed me, and at last I parted,
but my mind was almost altered from my first
purpose, from the trouble which I foresee in
wearing them also." Weeks passed before he
could make up his mind to wear a wig. Mrs
Pepys was taken to the periwig-maker's shop
to see the one made for Mr Pepys, and expressed
her satisfaction on seeing it. We read of the
wig being at Jervas's under repair in April 1665.
Early in May, Pepys writes in his "Diary," that
he suffered his hair to grow long, in order to wear
it ; but he said, "I will have it cut off all short
again, and will keep to periwigs." Later, under
date of September 3rd, he writes : "Lord's day.
Up ; and put on my coloured silk suit, very fine,
and my new periwig, bought a good while since,
but durst not wear, because the plague was in
Westminster when I bought it ; and it is a
wonder what will be in fashion, after the plague
is done, as to periwigs, for nobody will dare to
buy any hair, for fear of the infection, that it
had been cut off the heads of people dead of
the plague."

We learn from an entry in the "Diary" for
June 11th, 1666, that ladies, in addition to
assuming masculine costume for riding, wore
long wigs. "Walking in the galleries at Whitehall," observes Mr Pepys, "I find the ladies of

honour dressed in their riding garbs, with coats and doublets with deep skirts, just for all the world like mine, and buttoned their doublets up the breast, with periwigs and with hats, so that, only for long petticoats dragging under their men's coats, nobody could take them for women in any point whatever." Pepys, we have seen, wondered if periwigs would survive after the terrible plague. He thought not, but he was mistaken. Wigs still remained popular. The plague passed away, and its terrors were forgotten. The world of folly went on much as of yore, perhaps with greater gaiety, as a reaction to the lengthened time of depression.

The Earl of Albemarle.

In some instances the wig appears much out of place, and a notable example is that given in the portrait by Kneller, of George, Earl of Albemarle. He is dressed in armour, and wearing a long flowing wig. Anything more absurd could scarcely be conceived.

The beau of the period when the wig was popular carried in his pocket beautifully made combs, and in his box at the play, or in other places, combed his periwig, and rendered himself irresistible to the ladies. Making love seems to have been the chief aim of his life. Sir John Hawkins, in his " History of Music," published in 1776, has an informing note on combing customs. " On the Mall and in the theatre," he tells us, " gentlemen conversed and combed their perukes. There is now in being a fine picture by the elder Laroon of John, Duke of Marlborough, at his levée, in which his Grace is represented dressed in a scarlet suit, with large white satin cuffs, and a very long white peruke which he combs, while his valet, who stands behind him, adjusts the curls after the comb has passed through them." Allusions to this practice may be found in the plays from the reign of Charles II. down to the days of Queen Anne. We read in Dryden's prologue to " Almanzor and Almahide " :—-

"But as when vizard mask appears in pit,
   Straight every man who thinks himself a wit
   Perks up, and, managing a comb with grace,
   With his white wig sets off his nut-brown face."

Says Congreve, in the " Way of the World " :—

The gentlemen stay but to comb, madam, and will wait on you."

Thomas Brown, in his " Letters from the Dead to the Living," presents a pen-portrait of

beaux as they appeared at the commencement
of the eighteenth century. Some of the passages
are well worth re-
producing, as they
contain valuable in-
formation concern-
ing wigs. "We met,"
says the writer,
"three flaming
beaux of the first
magnitude. He in
the middle made a
most magnificent
figure—his periwig
was large enough
to have loaded a
camel, and he be-
stowed upon it at
least a bushel of
powder, I warrant
you. His sword-
knot dangled upon
the ground, and his
steinkirk, that was
most agreeably dis-
coloured with snuff
from the top to
the bottom, reach'd

Man with Wig and Muff, 1693
(*from a print of the period*).

down to his waist ; he carry'd his hat under his
left arm, walk'd with both hands in the waist-
band of his breeches, and his cane, that hung

negligently down in a string from his right arm, trail'd most harmoniously against the pebbles, while the master of it was tripping it nicely upon his toes or humming to himself." About this period in cold weather men wore muffs as well as wigs. A ballad, describing the frost fair on the Thames in the winter of 1683-84, mentions amongst those present :—

"A spark of the Bar with his cane and his muff."

Down to the middle of the eighteenth century wigs continued to increase in size. It will not now be without interest to direct attention to a few of the many styles of wigs. Randle Holme, in his "Academy of Armory," published in 1684, has some interesting illustrations, and we will draw upon him for a couple of pictures. Our first example is called the campaign - wig. He says it "hath knobs or bobs, or dildo, on each side, with a curled forehead." This is not so cumbrous as a periwig we have noticed. Another ex-ample from Holme is a

Campaign Wig.

smaller style of periwig with tail, and from this wig doubtless originated the familiar pig-tail. It was of various forms, and Swift says :—

"We who wear our wigs
With fantail and with snake."

F

A third example given by Holme is named the " short-bob," and is a plain peruke, imitating a natural head of hair. " Perukes," says Malcolm, in his " Manners and Customs," " were an highly

important article in 1734. Those of right gray human hair were four guineas each ; light grizzle ties, three guineas; and other colours in proportion, to twenty-five shillings. Right gray human hair, cue perukes, from two

Periwig with Tail.

guineas ; white, fifteen shillings each, which was the price of dark ones ; and right gray bob perukes, two guineas and a half ; fifteen shillings was the price of dark bobs. Those mixed with horsehair were much lower. It will be observed from the gradations in price, that real gray hair was most in fashion, and dark of no estimation." As time ran its course, wigs became more varied in form, and bore different names.

We find in the days of Queen Anne such designations as black riding-wigs, bag-wigs, and nightcap-wigs. These were in addition to the long, formally curled perukes. In 1706 the English, led by Marlborough, gained a great victory on the battlefield of Ramillies, and that gave the title to a long wig described as " having a long, gradually diminishing, plaited tail, called the ' Ramillie-tail,' which was tied with a great bow at the top, and a smaller one at the

bottom." It was at the great battle fought
before the town of Ramillies that France lost the
whole Spanish Netherlands, and Europe gained
a wig from the vanity of Louis XIV., of whom
Thackeray irreverently speaks in
his "Henry Esmond," as "a little,
wrinkled old man, pock-marked,
and with a great periwig and red
heels." Lord Lyttelton in his letters
thus refers to the French king :
" Louis XIV. annexed great dignity
to his peruke, which he increased to
an enormous size, and made a lion's
mane the object of its similitude.
That monarch, who daily studied
the part of a king, was never seen

Ramillie Wig.

uncovered but by the barber who shaved him.
It was not his practice to exchange his wig
for a nightcap till he was enclosed by his
curtains, when a page received the former from
his hand and delivered it to him in the morning
before he undrew them. The figure of the
great Bourbon must at times have been truly
ridiculous." It is stated in Read's *Weekly Journal*
of May 1st, 1736, in a report of the marriage
of the Prince of Wales, that " the officers of the
Horse and Foot Guards wore Ramillie periwigs
by His Majesty's order." This wig survived
until the days of George III. We meet, in the
reign of George II., other forms of the wig, and
more titles for them ; the most popular, perhaps,

was the pig-tail.   The pig-tails were worn hanging down the back, or tied up in a knot behind

as shown in our illustra-
tion.   This form of wig
was popular in the army,
but in 1804 orders were
given for it to be reduced
to seven inches in length,
and finally, in 1808, to be
cut off.   It is recorded
that when the Reform Bill
of 1832 received the Royal
assent, the Lord Bathurst

Pig-tail Wig.

of the period solemnly cut off his pig-tail,
saying, " Ichabod, for the glory was departed."

In the first reformed
Parliament   only   one
pig - tail   was   returned,
and that was Mr Shep-
pard, M.P. for Frome.

Here is a picture of
an ordinary man ; by
no means can he be re-
garded as a beau.   He
is wearing a common
bag-wig, dating back to
about the middle of the
eighteenth century.   The

Bag-Wig.

style is modified to suit an individual taste,
and for one who did not follow the extreme
fashion of his time.   In this example may be

observed the sausage curls over the ear, and the frizziness over the forehead.

We have directed attention to the large periwigs, and given a portrait of the Earl of Albemarle wearing one. In the picture of the House of Commons in the time of Sir Robert Walpole we get an excellent indication of how popular the periwig was amongst the lawmakers of the land. Farquhar, in a comedy called "Love and a Bottle," brought out in 1698, says, " A full wig is imagined to be as infallible a token of wit as the laurel."

Tillotson is usually regarded as the first amongst the English clergy to adopt the wig. He said in one of his sermons : " I can remember since the wearing of hair below the ears was looked upon as a sin of the first magnitude, and when ministers generally, whatever their text was, did either find or make occasion to reprove the great sin of long hair ; and if they saw any one in the congregation guilty in that kind, they would point him out particularly, and let fly at him with great zeal." Dr Tillotson died on November 24th, 1694. Wigs found favour with parsons, and in course of time they appear to have been indispensable. A volume, in 1765, was issued under the title of " Free Advice to a Young Clergyman," from the pen of the Rev. John Chubbe, in which he recommended the young preacher always to wear a full wig until age had made his own hair respectable. Dr

Randolph, on his advancement to the bishopric, presumed to wait upon George IV. to kiss hands without wearing a wig. This could not be over-looked by the king, and he said, " My lord, you must have a wig." Bishops wore wigs until the days of William IV. Bishop Blomfield is said to have been the first bishop to set the example of wearing his own hair. Even as late as 1858, at the marriage of the Princess Royal of England, Archbishop Sumner appeared in his wig.

Medical men kept up the custom of wearing wigs for a long period : perhaps they felt like a character in Fielding's farce, " The Mock Doctor," who exclaims, " I must have a physician's habit, for a physician can no more prescribe without a full wig than without a fee." The wig known as the full-bottomed wig was worn by the medical profession :—

> " Physic of old her entry made
> Beneath the immense, full-bottom'd shade ;
> While the gilt cane, with solemn pride
> To each suspicious nose applied,
> Seemed but a necessary prop
> To bear the weight of wig at top."

We are told Dr Delmahoy's wig was particularly celebrated in a song which commenced :—

> " If you would see a noble wig,
> And in that wig a man look big,
> To Ludgate Hill repair, my boy,
> And gaze on Dr Delmahoy."

In the middle of the last century so much importance was attached to this portion of a medical man's costume, that Dr Brocklesby's barber was in the habit of carrying a bandbox through the High Change, exclaiming : " Make way for Dr Brocklesby's wig ! "

Professional wigs are now confined to the Speaker in the House of Commons, who, when in the chair, wears a full-bottomed one, and to judges and barristers. Such wigs are made of horse-hair, cleaned and curled with care, and woven on silk threads, and shaped to fit the head with exactness. The cost of a barrister's wig of frizzed hair is from five to six guineas.

An eminent counsel in years agone wished to make a motion before Judge Cockburn, and in his hurry appeared without a wig. "I hear your voice," sternly said his Lordship, "but I cannot see you." The barrister had to obtain the loan of a wig from a learned friend before the judge would listen to him.

Lord Eldon suffered much from headache, and when he was raised to the peerage he petitioned the king to allow him to dispense with the wig. He was refused, his Majesty saying he could not permit such an innovation. In vain did his lordship show that the wig was an innovation, as the old judges did not wear them. "True," said the king ; "the old judges wore beards."

In more recent times we have particulars of several instances of both bench and bar discarding the use of the wig. At the Summer Assizes at Lancaster, in 1819, a barrister named Mr Scarlett hurried into court, and was permitted to take part in a trial without his wig and gown. Next day the whole of the members of the bar appeared without their professional badges, but only on this occasion, although on the previous day a hope had been expressed that the time was not far distant when the mummeries of costume would be entirely discarded.

We learn from a report in the *Times* of July 24th, 1868, that on account of the unprecedented heat of the weather on the day before, in the Court of Probate and Divorce the learned judge and bar appeared without wigs.

On July 22nd, 1873, it is recorded that Dr Kenealy rose to open the case for the defence in the Tichborne suit; he sought and obtained permission to remove his wig on account of the excessive heat.

Towards the close of the eighteenth century few were the young men at the Universities who ventured to wear their own hair, and such as did were designated Apollos. Women, as well as men, called into requisition, to add to their charms, artificial accessories in the form of wigs and curls. Ladies' hair was curled and frizzed with considerable care, and frequently false curls were worn under the name of heart-breakers. It will be seen from the illustration we give that these curls increased the beauty of a pretty face.

Queen Elizabeth, we gather from Hentzner and other authorities, wore false hair. We are told that ladies, in compliment to her, dyed their hair a sandy hue, the natural colour of the queen's locks.

It is recorded that Mary Queen of Scots

Heart-Breakers.

obtained wigs from Edinburgh not merely while in Scotland, but during her long and weary captivity in England. From "The True Report of the Last Moments of Mary Stuart," it appears that when the executioner lifted the head by the hair to show it to the spectators, it fell from his hands owing to the hair being false.

We have previously mentioned Pepys' allusions to women and wigs in 1666. Coming down to later times, we read in the *Whitehall Evening Post* of August 17th, 1727, that when the King, George II., reviewed the Guards, the three eldest

With and Without a Wig.

Princesses "went to Richmond in riding habits, with hats, and feathers, and periwigs."

It will be seen from the picture of a person with and without a wig that its use made a plain face presentable. There is a good election story of Daniel O'Connell. It is related during a fierce debate on the hustings, O'Connell with his biting witty tongue, attacked his opponent on account of his ill-favoured countenance. But, not to be outdone, and thinking to turn the gathering against O'Connell, his adversary called out, "Take off your wig, and I'll warrant that you'll prove the uglier." The witty Irishman immediately responded, amidst roars of laughter from the crowd, by snatching the wig from off his own head and exposing to view a bald pate, destitute of a single hair. The relative question of beauty was scarcely settled by this amusing rejoinder, but the laugh was certainly on O'Connell's side.

An interesting tale is told of Peter the Great of Russia. In the year 1716, the famous Emperor was at Dantzig, taking part in a public ceremony, and feeling his head somewhat cold, he stretched out his hand, and seizing the wig from the head of the burgomaster sitting below him, he placed it on his own regal head. The surprise of the spectators may be better imagined than described. On the Czar returning the wig, his attendants explained that his Majesty was in the habit of borrowing the wig of any nobleman within reach on similar occasions. His Majesty, it may be added, was short of hair.

Wigs were not confined to men. At the commencement of the eighteenth century little boys attended school in wigs and cocked hats. "Had I lived in the reign of good Queen Anne," wrote Lord Lyttelton, "my baby face must have been adorned with a full-bottomed periwig as large as that which bedecks the head and shoulders of

Mr Justice Blackstone when he scowls at the unhappy culprit who is arraigned before him." We learn from Miss Agnes Strickland that "Marie Antoinette was the first person who broke the absurd fashion of dressing infant boys as droll miniatures of their fathers. She attired the unfortunate Dauphin in a simple blue jacket and trousers, for which she was reviled, as if little bag-wigs and tiny cocked-hats, and all the paraphernalia of full dress, had been points of moral obligation. There are noblemen yet in existence," she says, when writing her history, "who can remember, at six years old, joining the juvenile parties given by George III. and Queen Charlotte, dressed after the models of their fathers' court costumes, with powdered side-curls, single-breasted coat, knee-buckles, and shoe-buckles."

It will not be without interest to give a picture of a full-bottomed wig, and we select as an example the one worn by the great Lord Mansfield. It was made by Mr Williams, a noted barber in his day, who had among his patrons many famous men, including Dr Samuel Johnson, but he prided himself most on making the full state wig for Lord Mansfield, and the one which is represented on his imposing monument in Westminster Abbey. After the famous lawyer had been laid to rest, the wig which is represented on his monument was the subject of a very odd litigation, which was fully reported in the *Times* for

1823. An action, it is stated, was brought by Mr Williams, a barber, against Mr Lawrence, to recover Lord Mansfield's full state wig, which had again come into the possession of the perruquier after the death of his lordship. The wig had been graciously lent by the barber to one Lawrence, belonging to the legal profession, but also an amateur actor. In this wig, we are told, he proposed to disport himself in the character of Shylock. The plaintiff could not get

Lord Mansfield.

it back again, and brought the action for its recovery. The wig had been accidentally burnt, and the judge awarded the plaintiff the sum of £2 as a compensation for the loss of the relic.

STEALING WIGS

N the palmy days of wigs the price of a full-wig of an English gentleman was from thirty to forty guineas. Street quarrels in the olden time were by no means uncommon ; care had to be exercised that wigs were not lost. Swift says :—

"Triumphing Tories and desponding Whigs,
    Forget their feuds, and join to save their wigs."

Although precautions were taken to prevent
wigs being stolen, we are told that robberies

Stealing a Wig.

were frequently committed. Sam Rogers thus
describes a successful mode of operation: "A
boy was carried covered over in a butcher's
tray by a tall man, and the wig was twisted off
in a moment by the boy. The bewildered
owner looked all round for it, when an accom-
plice impeded his progress under the pretence

of assisting him while the tray-bearer made off."
Gay, in *Trivia*, thus writes :—

> " Nor is the flaxen wig with safety worn :
> High on the shoulders in a basket borne
> Lurks the sly boy, whose hand, to rapine bred,
> Plucks off the curling honours of thy head."

THE WIG-MAKERS' RIOT

N February 11th, 1765, a curious
spectacle was witnessed in the streets
of London, and one which caused
some amusement.   Fashion had
changed ; the peruke was no longer in favour, and
only worn to a limited extent.   A large number
of peruke-makers had been thrown out of employ-
ment, and distress prevailed amongst them.   The
sufferers thought that help might be obtained
from George III., and a petition was accordingly
drawn up for the enforcement of gentlefolk
to wear wigs for the benefit of the wig-makers.
A procession was formed, and waited upon the
king at St James's Palace.   His Majesty, it is
said, returned a gracious answer, but it must
have cost him considerable effort to maintain his
gravity.

Besides the monarch, the unemployed had to
encounter the men of the metropolis, and we
learn from a report of the period they did not

fare so well. "As the distressed men went processionally through the town," says the account, "it was observed that most of the wig-makers, who wanted other people to wear them, wore no wigs themselves; and this striking the London mob as something monstrously unfair and inconsistent, they seized the petitioners, and cut off all their hair per force."

Horace Walpole alludes to this ludicrous petition in one of his letters. "Should we wonder," he writes, "if carpenters were to remonstrate that since the Peace there is no demand for wooden legs?" The wags of the period could not allow the opportunity to pass without attempting to provoke more mirth out of the matter, and a petition was published purporting to come from the body-carpenters imploring his Majesty to wear a wooden leg, and to enjoin his servants to appear in his royal presence with the same graceful decoration.

THE MOUSTACHE MOVEMENT

T the present time, when moustaches are general, it is difficult to realise the opposition raised against them in this country half a century ago. Few outside the military had the courage to follow a fashion which has become general.

In the first year of the reign of Queen Victoria, we gather from the police court proceedings at Marlborough Street, London, how unpopular at that period was the moustache. The following Report is drawn from the *Times* of September 21st, 1837 : " Yesterday, a young man, ' bearded like the pard,' who said he was a carpenter employed on the London and Birmingham Railroad, applied to Mr Rawlinson, the sitting magistrate, for an assault warrant, under the following ludicrous circumstances.

" Mr Rawlinson : What do you want a warrant for ?

" Applicant : I'll tell your worship, and you'll say it's the most haggrawating, and provoking thing as ever was heard on. Vell then, I goes to my vork, as usual, this 'ere morning, ven one of my shopmates said to me, ' Bill, you arn't shaved your hupper lip lately,' says I. ' Vy,' says he. ' Cos,' I replied, ' I intends vearing mustachios to look like a gentleman,' ' Vell, then,' says he, ' as you intends to become a fashionable gentleman, p'raps you'll have no objection to forfeit half-a-gallon of ale, as it's the rule here that every workman vot sports mustachios, to have them vetted a bit.' Vell, has I refused to have my mustachios christened, they made game of them, and said they weren't half fledged ; and, more nor all that, they hustled me about, and stole my dinner out of the

G

pot, and treated me shameful, and so I want your advice respecting my mustachios.

" Mr Rawlinson: My advice is, go to the barber and have them shaved off without loss of time.

" Applicant : Can't part with a single hair.

" Mr Rawlinson : You want to look like a grenadier, I suppose ?

" Applicant: My granny-dear (God bless her dear old soul !), she never had such a fashionable and warlike appendage in her life.

" Mr Rawlinson: What business has a carpenter with a quantity of long hair hanging from his lip?

" Applicant : The reason vy I rears it is 'cos it's fashionable, and makes me look like a man of some courage.

" Mr Rawlinson : Fashionable, indeed ! I wish, with all my heart, that the fashion was discontinued.   Why need an Englishman make a Jew of himself?   It is disgusting to see persons strutting through the streets with mustachios, and sometimes a fringe of hair round the face and chin, which is dignified by the name of whiskers.   As you won't take my advice, I can't assist you.

" Applicant : Vot ! not for striking me on the hupper lip ?

" Mr Rawlinson : Then your moustachios must have saved you.

" Applicant : No, they didn't.

" Mr Rawlinson : How's that ?

" Applicant : 'Cos the hair ain't long and thick enough ; they're only young 'uns as yet. There was no occasion to strike me.

" Mr Rawlinson : And there's no occasion for you to wear mustachios. You may have a warrant if you like, but I think you had better not."

" The man with the mustachios then withdrew."

About 1855 the beard movement took hold of Englishmen. The Crimean War had much to do with it, as our soldiers were permitted to forego the use of the razor as the hair on the face protected them from the cold and attacks of neuralgia. About this period only one civilian of position in England had the hardihood to wear the moustache. He was Mr George Frederick Muntz, a member of Parliament for Birmingham. He was a notable figure in the House of Commons, and is described as manly in appearance, with a handsome face, a huge black beard, and moustache. He died 30th July, 1857, and is regarded as the father of the modern moustache movement. Another early moustache member was Colonel Sibthorp, the representative for Lincoln, who bore Mr Muntz company for some time in the House of Commons. Daniel O'Connell wrote a biting epigram on Colonels Sibthorp, Percival, and Verner, the first of whom was remarkable for his length of beard, whilst the others had none :—

Three Colonels, in three distant counties born,
Lincoln, Armagh, and Sligo did adorn.
The first in matchless impudence surpass'd,
The next in bigotry, in both the last,
The force of nature could no further go,
To beard the first she shaved the other two.

George Frederick Muntz, M.P.

It will be noticed that the foregoing is a parody on Dryden's celebrated tribute to Milton.

The enlightened electors, however, did not take kindly to the bearded politician. It is related by Dr Hedderwick, the well-known Glasgow journalist, that at the time the moustache movement was making slow progress, the candidate for Linlithgowshire was an officer in the Lancers, a man of ability, family, and fashion, who wore a heavily hirsute upper lip. He received an intimation from a leader of his party that his moustache might prejudice him in the eyes of a rural population. The candidate replied that he had already considered the point, but it was the rule in his regiment that it would be cowardly to succumb, and that he was " determined to face it out."

We have it on good authority that a Cabinet Minister, about 1855, caused a gentleman to be told that the beard and moustache did not look well on a man holding a civic position under the Crown. This Minister did not then imagine that shortly men with beards and moustaches would sit by his side as members of the Cabinet. Even a Colonial Governor about half a century ago was not supposed to wear a moustache. Dr Hedderwick, in his " Backward Glances" (Edinburgh, 1891), tells us that on a certain Sunday he was rambling with his friend, Mr Charles Maclaren, the well-known editor of the *Scotsman*, to Loch Long, when he saw some carriages conveying a number of ladies and gentlemen to church. " Sitting obliquely on an Irish jaunting-car," says the doctor, " was a portly personage with a dark heavy fringe on his upper lip, and otherwise distinguished appearance. I suggested that it might be Sir Henry Pottinger, the celebrated diplomatist and Colonial Governor. We knew he had returned to England, and I had heard he was visiting in Scotland on the banks of Loch Long. "No, no," said Mr Maclaren, "it's quite impossible it can be he. A civilian of great intelligence and sense would never wear a moustache." We may gather from the foregoing the prejudice of the period against facial adornments.

From about 1855 to some years afterwards we resided at the small town of Alfreton, Derbyshire, where, if by chance the boys saw a man with a moustache, with one accord they commenced calling after him, "Jew, Jew, Jew," or "Frenchy, Frenchy, Frenchy," and, if that did not make any impression, they commenced stoning the offender against the unwritten laws of the land. In later years our barber at Wakefield was somewhat of a dandy, and would, perhaps, have preferred being called a tonsorial artist. He was the first to cultivate a moustache in that West Riding town, and he told the writer with pride that in those distant days he was one of the sights of the place, but his vanity had many checks from the rough lads, and even men, of Wakefield. Before his death he saw many follow his lead.

A teacher of music was the first to wear a

moustache in Nottingham. He attracted the attention of young and old, and was deemed a great curiosity. The younger generation made matters lively for the music master. Speaking on this theme to an old Nottinghamshire friend, with whom we often discuss olden days and ways, he stated to us how he won his wife because he had not a moustache. It appears another eligible young man was anxious to win the young lady, but his character was regarded as doubtful because he cultivated a moustache. After a short engagement our friend was married in the year 1855. At this period the moustache movement was making slow progress in Nottingham.

Mr W. P. Frith, R.A., published in 1887 an amusing " Autobiography," and devotes not the least attractive chapter of his work to " The Bearded Model." He relates how difficult it was to find a bearded model, and how at last he discovered one. He says that in crossing Soho Square one day his attention was drawn to a crowd of little boys, who seemed to be teasing an old man in the manner of the London street boy. " Why don't you get your 'air cut ? " said one. " Yah ! where's your bundle of old clothes ? Yer ain't got 'em in that 'ere basket, 'ave you ? " said another. " Let's 'ave a look. You're a Jew, you know ; now, ain't you ? " and so on. All this, observes the artist, because the old man wore a long grey beard, then such a rarity. The young gentlemen had mistaken their man. He soundly punished two elder boys, and Mr Frith found he was not a Jew. How he became a model does not come within the scope of our present studies.

Mr Frith says that the head of a well-known firm of drapers in Regent Street refused to employ shopmen who wore moustaches, or men who parted their hair down the middle. In days before the moustache was popular, Mr Frith shows how even in art circles its adoption retarded progress. " I well remember," says Mr Frith, " a book illustrator named Stuart, who, according to his own notion, ought to have been on the throne of England, instead of drawing on insensible wood blocks. He could trace his descent from James I. He could sing Jacobite songs, and very well, too, and he was certainly like Charles I. There was not the least doubt about his pedigree in his own mind ; and he was such a nuisance when once launched into the long list of Royal blood, that we declared our unanimous conviction of the justice of his claims, and implored him to put them forward in the proper quarter, as we were powerless in the matter. The Stuart beard, exactly like the Vandyke portrait of Charles, was the treasured ornament of our friend's face, and though he was assured that the publishers felt such doubt of his abilities, and such a conviction of his utterly unreliable character and

general dishonesty in consequence of his beard
—one man going so far as to tell him it cost
him £200 a year—he refused to remove it."
Mr Frith says when the Vandyke beard became
white his poor friend would have died in extreme poverty had he not received well-deserved
assistance from a fund established to meet cases
like his.

The directors and managers of banks made a
stand against the moustache movement. It is
asserted that the authorities of the Bank of
England issued an order " that the clerks were
not to wear moustaches during business hours."
It is not surprising to learn that the amusing
order was soon cancelled. At the present time,
at one of the great banks in the Strand, the
clerks have to be clean shaven. To illustrate
the rigid manner of enforcing the order, Mr
Frith quotes the case of an old servant of the
bank, who was severely attacked by erysipelas
in the face and head. Even after convalescence
the tenderness of the skin made shaving impossible, but the old clerk begged to be allowed
to return to his desk. He was told by one of
the principals, in a kind note in answer to his
application, that the bank would endeavour to
get on without him until his face was in a condition to bear the attention of his razor.

In the earlier years of the moustache movement, clerks might be dismissed for not being
clean shaven. Contractors, as a rule, we should

regard as being the least particular of any class of employers about the personal appearance of their servants. Yet we have it on reliable authority that a trusted superintendent of one of

the great contractors served the firm in Russia, and there cultivated the beard and moustache. On his return to England he displayed no disposition to resume the use of the razor. The head contractor grew alarmed at the terrible example he was setting those engaged in the

Charles Dickens, born 1812, died 1870.

office, and insisted that the adornment should be cut off, which was done. The poor fellow caught cold, and in a few days died.

An important firm of timber merchants in Hull made it a condition that any clerks employed by them should be clean shaven. This rule was strictly enforced until the firm closed its career a few years ago.

Mr Serjeant Robinson, in his interesting and informing volume, "Bench and Bar Reminis-

cences" (London, 1889), deals with the legal
aspect of our theme. He says for many years
anterior to 1860 scarcely a beard, and certainly
not even a downy symptom of a moustache, was
to be seen on the face of a practising barrister.
Towards the close of the first half of the nineteenth century a quiet, gentlemanly, well-
informed barrister, named Brierley, used to
attend the Central Criminal Court, wearing a
long flowing beard and a thick moustache.
These hirsute adornments gave offence to the
leaders who regularly attended the sessions.
No other exception could be taken to him. A
meeting of the senior Bar was held, and he was
summoned to attend. He was called upon to
defend his action. Instead of denying the juris-
diction of the tribunal that was to judge him, he
recognised the enormity of his crime, and
excused himself on the ground of a serious
affection of the throat, and stated that it was
under urgent medical advice that he was induced
to transgress the unwritten ordinances of the
Bar. Despite the reasonableness of the plea,
a small majority passed upon him a vote of
censure for subjecting the Bar to general ridicule
by his extravagant physiognomy. "This was,"
says Mr Serjeant Robinson, "the worst that
could befall him, for of course he could not be
prevented from coming within the sacred pre-
cincts of the court, nor from taking his seat at
the Bar table. The only means of carrying out

the resolution was by sending him to Coventry. But he did not give them the opportunity of executing it, for he seldom appeared afterwards. It is not known what became of this barrister after he had been driven from practising his profession in the courts."

Several old laws regulated wearing the beard in the bygone times. In the reign of Queen Elizabeth a decree went forth that no barrister should appear in court with a beard of more than a fortnight's growth.

Barristers with beards and moustaches are not much less common at the present time than those without them.   This is no doubt the result of the martial order which passed over the country at the introduction of the Volunteer movement. The moustache was regarded as indispensable to the military appearance of the citizen soldier.

Old illustrated books relating to the worthies of the Church often contain portraits of divines with flowing beards and moustaches.   In modern times the cultivation of these adornments of the face has given rise to not a little discussion in Church circles.   Early in 1861 the newspapers criticised the charge of the Bishop of Rochester, which included a denunciation of the develop-ment of beards and moustaches among the clergymen of his diocese. The writing in the press for and against the facial adornment had little point, but it gave rise to more than one book dealing with the subject. An author issued " An Apology for the Beard ; addressed to men in general, and to the clergy in particular " (London, 1862). The Bible and other books are quoted against shaving. James Ward, R.A., the celebrated animal painter, produced in book form a " Defence of the Beard." He dealt with his subject on scriptural grounds, and gave eighteen reasons why man was bound to grow a beard unless he was indifferent as to offending his Creator and good taste. Mr. Ward asked, " What would a Jupiter be without a beard ? Who would countenance the idea of a shaved Christ ? " The artist set an example to others by adopting the beard when it was not popular. On the title-page of another work was declared : " A Breach of the Sabbath, and a Hindrance to the Spread of the Gospel." The writer designated himself " Theologos." If his views were carried out, it would lead to the practice which prevailed among the Essenes, who never did on the Sabbath anything that was customary for them to do on other days. The High Church clergymen use the razor, and as a rule the moustache is discarded. For some time not a few of the clergy in the lower ranks joined the moustache movement, but it was not until 1889 that a bishop was included. The late Bishop Ryle, of Liverpool, was the first to give up in modern times the use of the razor. Quite a sensation was caused towards the close of 1892 when it became known that the Archbishop of York did not approve of the moustache among his clergy. In several quarters the barber was visited, and the cherished moustache and beard swept away, it is said, to please the head of the Church in the Northern Province. Not so with a moustached candidate for Orders from Hull. He had been spending two or three days at Bishopthorpe before ordination, but gentle hints failed to induce him to make a clean shave. As a final effort the chaplain of the Archbishop asked him if he thought it was not time he cut off his moustache. He replied that he did not think of doing so, and asked why he should. "Well," said the chaplain, "you see the saints in the stained glass windows have not any moustaches." "That may be so," said the candidate, "but as I am not intended to be a saint and stuck in a window, I mean my moustache to remain."

Speaking at a reunion of the Leeds Clergy School held on June 6th, 1899, Dr Eden, the Bishop of Wakefield, said he recently noticed a paragraph in the newspapers which said that the Bishop of Wakefield had given it out that he was very much against the clergy wearing moustaches. "After a little while this legend increased in definiteness, and the next paragraph I saw was that the Bishop of Wakefield had 'commanded' the curates of his diocese to shave clean. A little while after that I took

up a London paper, and I saw it stated : ' The
Bishop of Wakefield has joined the anti-
moustache brigade, and we believe he has the
sympathy of His Royal Highness the Prince of
Wales.'   I waited a little longer, for I felt sure
something more would come, and then I took
up another paper and found that an exceedingly
respected Prebendary of St Paul's in London
had been uttering remarks, either in public or
to the reporters—I don't know which—in which
he held up the Bishop of Wakefield as being
one of those foolish people who had largely
exceeded their episcopal powers.   I was given
a very round lecture upon the contrast of my
conduct with that of my predecessor, who would
never have thought of issuing such a foolish
order to the curates to shave their moustaches.
The curates were recommended to do nothing
of the kind, but a fear was expressed that a
large number of them would probably comply
with the demand.   Still that was not quite the
end of the legend ; I had of course a great deal
of private correspondence arising out of this
newspaper paragraph, but only the other day
I heard—I have not seen it—that a cartoon
has appeared in a London paper in which the
Bishop of Wakefield is represented with a drawn
razor in his hand in full cry after a Wakefield
curate with a moustache.   That is a very good
example of finding the truth about yourselves
in the newspapers, for I have the most as-

tounding fact of all to tell you, and that is that I have never said a single word about moustaches from first to last. I knew you would forgive me making this little personal reference because it is not personal to myself and to many of those in this tent."

A former Bishop of Wakefield, Dr Walsham How, related a good story. "The vicar of an East London parish," said the bishop, "was one of the first London clergymen to grow his beard. The then Bishop of London wished to stop the practice, and, as he was going to confirm in that church, sent his chaplain to the vicar to ask him to shave it off, saying he should otherwise select another church for the Confirmation. The vicar replied that he was quite willing to take his candidates to another church, and would give out next Sunday the reason for the change. Of course the bishop retracted."

We are told in the "Life of R. W. Dale" (London, 1898) that this famous Birmingham preacher, about 1860, was clean shaven, but with "long black hair that hung over his cheeks and ears like a mane." In a year or two it was cut short. He then let his beard grow, and, after some hesitation, his moustache. Many of the older people, we are told, were scandalised, but remained silent ; some wrote to the newspapers in protest. The moustache was declared to invest ministers "with an air of levity and worldliness." A letter of approval purported to

come from the shade of a Wesleyan minister,
the Rev. H. D. Lowe, who, in 1828, had his
beard cut off by order of the Wesleyan Confer-
ence.   It ran as follows :—

" REVEREND AND BEARDED SIR,—It rejoiced
my shade to see you not only addressing
Methodists, but sitting among many of the
identical men who required that cruel sacrifice
of me, and that unrebuked when you even spoke
of dreaming of belonging to the ' Legal Hundred,'
bearded though you are."

Professor Hodgson used to tell a good story
of a shaky village knight of the razor who
gashed the minister's cheek.   " John, John ! "
cried the reverend sufferer, " it's a dreadful thing
that drink ! "   " 'Deed it is, sir," mildly as-
sented John, " it makes the skin unco tender."

The electors of Hull, who returned to Parliament Sir Henry Vane the younger, Andrew
Marvell, the patriot, and in later times, William
Wilberforce, the emancipator of the slave, have
never, as might be readily believed, been backward in adopting reasonable measures of reform.
On December 1st, 1859, at the Hull Watch
Sub-Committee, it was moved by Mr Moss,
seconded by Mr Clarke, and carried unanimously :
" That it be a recommendation to the Watch
Committee to permit the police to wear a beard
and moustache if they think fit."   A week
later, namely, on December 7th, at the Watch

H

Committee, it was moved by Mr Mayfield, and seconded by Mr Fountain : " That a resolution of the Sub-Committee of December 1st, granting permission to police to wear the beard and moustache, if they think fit, be confirmed by this Committee." It was pointed out by one of the members of the Council, who was advocating the passing of the resolution, that it would give a " fierce appearance to the police."

In course of time the leading gentlemen of the land adopted the moustache, and those in the lower walks of life were not slow to follow their example, the result being that it is worn now by all sorts and conditions of men.

The moustache figures in recent wills. In 1862 one made by Henry Budd came into force, and declared as follows against the wearing of moustaches by his sons in the following terms : " In case my son Edward shall wear moustaches, the devise hereinbefore contained in favour of him, his appointees, heirs, and assigns of my said estate, called Pepper Park, shall be void ; and I devise the same estate to my son William, his appointees, heirs, and assigns. And in case my said son William shall wear moustaches, then the devise hereinbefore contained in favour of him, his appointees, heirs, and assigns of my said estate, called Twickenham Park, shall be void ; and I devise the said estate to my said son Edward, his appointees, heirs, and assigns."

Mr Fleming, an upholsterer, of Pimlico, by

his will, proved in 1869, left £10 each to the men in his employ who did not wear moustaches, and to those who persisted in wearing them, £5 only.

In the daily newspapers of July 11th, 1901, it was stated: "French motor-car owners having shown a disposition to make their chauffeurs shave, the latter combined in defence of their moustaches, which they declare to be a sanitary protection."

INDEX